THE ENGLISH REFORMATION

*From Tragic Reality
to Dramatic Representation*

Peter Milward SJ

THE ENGLISH REFORMATION

From Tragic Reality
to Dramatic Representation

FAMILY PUBLICATIONS
OXFORD

ISBN 978-1-871217-71-1

published by
Family Publications
6a King Street, Oxford OX2 6DF, UK
www.familypublications.co.uk

Cover picture:
Henry VIII, Edward VI and the Pope (Unknown artist)
© National Portrait Gallery, London

Printed in England by
Cromwell Press, Trowbridge, Wilts

CONTENTS

PREFACE

"Do you really wish to know what is happening in the world today?" I ask my Japanese students. "Then you have to understand the West. After all, without any boasting, or rather much to my shame, it is out of the West that almost everything happening in the world today has come. The poor East is caught between the two extremes of the West, America and now China – after having long been Soviet Russia. Then, if you really wish to understand the West, it isn't enough to read newspapers about the present situation of the world. You have to study the history of the past few centuries, since as Confucius wisely observes, 'It is by studying the past that we know the present.'"

"But there's so much in the past for us to study," my poor students complain. "There are so many facts contained in books of history, and they only leave us confused. How can we know which facts are the important ones? How can we find our way in such a vast forest of facts?"

"Well," I say, "if you look at the facts, instead of complaining about them, you will find that there is one great turning-point in the history of the West. It is the turning-point that marks the change, or what is called the Great Divide, between the mediaeval past and the modern present. That is, without any doubt, the Reformation that took place in the sixteenth century. Mind you, I don't say the Renaissance, which was mainly a movement of artists and scholars. It may have seemed critical of the previous age in certain respects, but it was for the most part a development out of what we call the Middle Ages. So when we consider poets like Dante or painters like Fra Angelico, we find there is something of both ages in their inspiration. In them we see not any division or discontinuity but rather a continuity between the end of the one age and the beginning of the other. We may even say that the Renaissance had its roots in the Middle Ages, even extending as far as their beginnings in the decline of the Roman Empire.

"On the other hand," I continue, "when we turn from the Renaissance to the Reformation, we note a real and intentional break with the past, a break not just on the intellectual or the aesthetic level but on almost every level of ordinary life. It affected not just a few scholars or monks or artists but almost everyone in their everyday lives. Once the Reformation had established itself in Europe, there arose a different way of looking at human beings and the world, not to mention God himself, and that not only among the Protestants who accepted the new teaching of Luther and then Calvin, but also among the Catholics who opposed them. One living in 1550 could hardly help seeing life differently from one who had been living in 1500, even if he happened to be the same individual who had lived through the intervening years."

Then, turning my attention from Europe in general to England in particular, I continue: "If this is true of all Europe, as forming what was once called 'Christendom', it is true in a special way of England. If you wish to understand the English today, their character, their culture, their language and their literature, you have by all means to go back to the English Reformation and see what took place then. You have to study the reigns of Henry VIII and his daughter Elizabeth I, and see what principally moved them in their fateful decisions. If you think of it as just an affair of religion, you will be wrong. Yes, it was to some extent a religious reformation, but it was more than just an affair of religion. Or rather, you have to realize that in those days, for those people, religion was everything. It entered into and affected every activity of life. Just because Henry VIII got tired of his first wife, Catherine of Aragon, and the Pope wouldn't grant him the divorce he had requested, he took the matter into his own hands and so brought about a schism or separation from Rome. But that wasn't all. Much more was involved in the taking of such a step than even Henry himself realized at the time. What was involved was a complete break with the mediaeval past of England and with the Catholic countries of Europe, who now became England's potential enemies."

This is what I always tell my students in my various classes on Shakespeare and on English Thinkers, as well as in open lectures on Christianity and Literature. Needless to say, it isn't enough for me to utter all this in general terms. I have to show what the English Reformation was in detail. I have to show that it wasn't limited to the single issue of the King's divorce, which was at the time called "the King's great matter", but that there were many other issues also involved. The political issue may have been prominent in the minds of such rulers as Henry himself and Elizabeth. They both wished to be independent of papal authority and to be free to rule their kingdom according to their own desires, at least within the limits of English endurance. But in the minds of their principal supporters the liturgical and doctrinal issues figure no less prominently. First, there was the desire for an English liturgy, based on an English translation of the Bible, so that English people might be able to pray in their own language, and this desire led in turn to a new emphasis on the Bible rather than the Church as the final authority in matters of belief. Thus the religious division came to appear as one between the Catholic appeal to the Church and the Protestant appeal to the Bible. This wasn't just a religious division, but given the conditions of the age it came to appear also as a political division, especially when the Catholics under Elizabeth came to be discriminated against and openly persecuted not as heretics but as traitors to their country.

Finally, from the viewpoint of the literature and drama of the age, especially under Elizabeth, it is important to realize that this is the situation in which the so-called Elizabethan Renaissance came to flourish. It is, above all, the religious background to the drama of Shakespeare, in which it is customary to discern a development from comedy to tragedy and then back to tragi-comedy. These plays of his interestingly lead up to the history play of *Henry VIII*, though it wasn't entirely Shakespeare's. It begins with a Prologue, warning spectators of tragic events about to be presented:

I come no more to make you laugh. Things now
That bear a weighty and a serious brow,
Sad, high and working, full of state and woe,
Such noble scenes as make the eye to flow,
We now present.

Yet, though the dramatist goes on to present the political downfalls of such great figures as the Duke of Buckingham and Cardinal Wolsey, and the personal downfall of Catherine with the corresponding rise of Anne Boleyn, he is strangely silent about the great tragedy of the reign as a whole. Yet for this very reason one may say that for those who know, as we say, "Silence speaks louder than words."

Here then, in the circumstances of his age we may find a precious clue to a hidden meaning in Shakespeare's plays, just as in those plays we may also find a precious clue to the meaning not just of their age but of all subsequent ages. Then from little England, as interpreted by the universal genius of Shakespeare, we may look, as he also looks in his plays, to the wide world. It is perhaps significant that in his plays he never deals explicitly with his own age and nation, Elizabethan England, but he is always directing his eyes to exotic lands in Europe, Asia and Africa, and even in his last tragi-comedy *The Tempest* in America. It is as if he is looking to those lands for some measure of imaginative relief from the real misery he can't help seeing and lamenting in the England of his own time, though in his tragedies, above all in *King Lear*, he can't help betraying his real feelings. Thus it is with Shakespeare that I bring my analysis of these issues of the English Reformation to an end. Then, to use the dying words of Hamlet, "The rest is silence."

PART I – FIVE ISSUES

Chapter 1

THE POLITICAL ISSUE
THE KING'S MATTER

It is necessary for me to begin with a warning. The popularly accepted idea of the Reformation, as it took place in Germany and England in the sixteenth century, isn't necessarily true. To say the least, it is one-sided. It represents mainly one side, the Protestant side, in a very complicated series of events and issues. It is largely based on what is called the Whig interpretation of history as developed from the time of Gilbert Burnet, who published his *History of the Reformation in England* in three volumes from 1679 to 1714.

According to this interpretation, the Middle Ages formed a dark period in the history of Europe. It was a period of repression under the authority of the papacy, exercised through the complicated structure of the hierarchical Church. Learning was largely in the hands of the priests, who found it in their vested interest to keep the people in ignorance. But towards the end of this period there appeared the light of a new age, both for the world at large and particularly for the Church. For the world the light was that of the Renaissance, with its return to the classical culture of Greece and Rome. For the Church the light was that of the Reformation, with its return to the Gospel of Jesus Christ as set forth in the Bible.

Already before the time of Gilbert Burnet we find the great Puritan poet John Milton reflecting on this new light in his prose pamphlet, *Of Reformation touching Church Discipline*, in 1641. In it he looks back over "so many dark ages, wherein the huge, overshadowing train of error had almost swept all the stars out of the firmament of the Church," and he is filled with wonder to see "how the bright and blissful reformation (by divine power) struck through the black and settled night of ignorance and antichristian tyranny." With regard to England in particular, he praises King Henry VIII in his subsequent pamphlet, *On the Doctrine and Discipline of Divorce*, in 1645. He was the King who by divine grace came to perceive "all the tyranny of Rome", and to have thus been "the beginner of a reformation to the whole kingdom, by first asserting into his familiar power the right of just divorce."

Moreover, well before the time of Milton, at the very beginning of Elizabeth's reign, we find John Jewel speaking in similar terms in his famous "challenge sermon" at Paul's Cross in 1559. In it he speaks of "this last age of the world", in which "it hath pleased almighty God of his great mercy in these our days to remove away all deformities and to restore again the holy mysteries to their first original." He therefore rejoices to see how "the glorious light of the Gospel of Christ is now so mightily spread abroad." Subsequently, in his *Apology of the Church of England*, published in 1562, he recalls, with evident reference to Luther, how "in the midst of the darkness of that age (forty years agone) first began to spring and to shine some one glimmering beam of truth, unknown at that time and unheard of."

Certainly, if one agrees with Luther and Jewel, Milton and Burnet, that is how the events of the Reformation may appear to the mind. But that is only one side, the Protestant side. Then, what about the other side, the Catholic side, if only to obtain a balanced view of the period as a whole?

For this purpose we have to go back to the time of Martin Luther himself and to his rejection of the Church's teaching on Indulgences in 1517. At that time it would have seemed but a minor issue, when he merely objected to the teaching that by the giving of alms for the building of the new St Peter's in Rome one might free the souls of the dead from the fires of Purgatory. It was indeed a minor issue, in the context of the whole of dogmatic theology, but in Luther's mind it was already connected with a much larger issue, his new interpretation of the Bible. This interpretation, which he found confirmed by Erasmus' publication of the Greek

New Testament (with a new Latin translation by Erasmus) in 1516, had largely grown out of St Paul's statement in Romans i.17, itself a quotation from the prophecy of Habacuc, "The just shall live by faith."

What, we may ask, is the connection between the minor issue of Indulgences and this major issue of Faith and Justification? It is because, relying on the teaching of St Paul in Romans and Galatians, Luther came to emphasize an opposition between Faith and Works with regard to Justification and Salvation. For him Faith alone was necessary, not Works. In particular, he objected to the mediaeval insistence on the various works of piety, such as monastic prayer, devotion to Our Lady and the saints, pilgrimages to saints' shrines, Masses for the dead, as well as Indulgences. In this way, from the special issue of Indulgences he was led into a position at variance with that of the mediaeval Church as a whole.

This conflict came into the open in 1520, when Luther published a series of highly provocative pamphlets, two in his native German and one in Latin. In German he published *An Appeal to the Christian Nobility of the German Nation*, urging the German princes to support his proposals of reform, and a treatise *On the Liberty of a Christian Man*, maintaining that true freedom is based on faith and exempts human beings from the obligation of works. In Latin he published a theological treatise, *On the Babylonish Captivity of the Church*, rejecting the whole visible, hierarchical Church with its seven sacraments and other ceremonies. The response of Rome was inevitable and immediate. Pope Leo X condemned this new teaching as heretical in the bull *Exsurge Domine* in June 1520, and in the following January 1521 Luther was formally excommunicated.

From the beginning Luther received considerable support within his own nation, from both princes and people, not so much for theological reasons as for his appeal to national feeling. It was significant that two of these three pamphlets were in German, written in a popular style, and they were multiplied by the relatively new invention of printing. They also appealed to many German rulers as affording a new theoretical basis for independence from

Rome and for control over the Church within their dominions.

Turning now from Germany to England, we find similar feelings of nationalism at work among the new Tudor rulers and their people. It had been a major aim of the first Tudor King, Henry VII, to increase the royal power by limiting that of his nobles and thereby centralizing the government. While this policy was continued under his son, Henry VIII, the latter achieved more popular power with his prodigality than his father had ever attained fiscal power with his miserliness. While he left the administration of the affairs of state in the capable hands of his Chancellor, Cardinal Wolsey, he devoted his attention to sport and splendour.

At the same time, the new King was outwardly religious, professing himself no less a devout son of the Church than his father had been. He was also, like his wife Catherine of Aragon, interested in the New Learning, and it was in the early years of his reign that the so-called "Oxford reformers", John Colet, Desiderius Erasmus and Thomas More (as identified by Frederic Seebohm in his famous book of that title in 1867), flourished in England. Unlike Luther, who rejected the very institution of the Church, these men aimed rather at a reformation of abuses within the Church. In particular, More was invited to enter the royal service, and when he eventually did so – after having weighed the pros and the cons of the matter in his *Utopia* (1516) – he was successively promoted to the King's privy council in 1518 and the knighthood in 1521.

The King's own reaction to Luther's rebellion against the Church was by no means affirmative but strongly negative. He was one of the first to come out against Luther with his Latin treatise *Assertio Septem Sacramentorum* in 1521, in reply to Luther's *De Captivitate Babylonica Ecclesiae*. It was maintained at the time that this was the King's own work, with but minor assistance in theological matters from his learned chaplain, John Fisher, Chancellor of Cambridge University, and in literary style from his humanist counsellor, Thomas More. In the same year he was rewarded by the Pope with the title of *Fidei Defensor*, or Defender of the Faith, which has been retained by his successors till the present day. This led to the first controversy of the Reformation in England, as Luther promptly replied with an abusive pamphlet *Contra Henricum Regem Anglicum* in 1522, to which More responded on the King's behalf with a longer work in Latin, *Responsio ad Lutherum* (1523) under the pseudonym of Rossaeus.

From this time onwards we find Luther gaining disciples in England, especially from a group of young men at Cambridge University, who had been more or less directly influenced by the lectures given by Erasmus on the New Testament during his stay there from 1511 to 1514. The leader of these English Lutherans came to be William Tyndale in virtue of his pioneering work as translator of the New Testament into English, which was printed at Cologne and Worms in 1525. This gave rise to a further controversy with Thomas More, this time in English, in a series of books by the latter beginning with his *Dialogue Against Heresies* in 1528, and continuing even during his busy years as Chancellor in succession to Cardinal Wolsey.

It was also More who persuaded his friend Erasmus to come into the open against Luther. Till then Erasmus had been non-committal in his attitude to these early controversies, even to the extent of seeming to side with the reformers. Thus the Anglican Thomas Cooper, writing at the beginning of Elizabeth's reign, recalls how Erasmus had been esteemed as "a man of excellent learning and a singular instrument provided of God to begin the reformation of the Church in this latter time" (*An Apology*, 1562). By this time, however, Erasmus had become alienated from the reformers in view of their excesses in both words and deeds. "Look upon this evangelical people," he exclaimed, "and mark whether there be among them less riot, less sensuality, less covetousness, than there is among their Papist opponents." Hence in 1524 he published his treatise *De Libero Arbitrio* in defence of the Catholic teaching on free will against Luther's assertion of the corruption of human nature by original sin. In his response *De Servo Arbitrio*, published the following year, Luther admitted that this was the basic point of his reforming movement.

Coming at length to the main issue of this chapter, we may turn to the question how Henry VIII came to associate himself with the cause of reformation in England. In doctrinal matters he was from the outset firmly opposed to both Luther and Tyndale, regarding himself as a Catholic, even more Catholic than the Pope. In political matters, however, he was led to agree with them against the Pope. Luther's appeal to the German princes against the claims of the papacy found a responsive echo in the heart of Henry, especially when stated in English form by William Tyndale in his *Obedience of a Christian Man* (1528). In this book Tyndale expressed his opinion that ". . . the King is in this world without law and may at his lust do right or wrong and shall give account but to God only." When Henry read these words, pointed out to him by his minister, Thomas Cromwell, he remarked, "This book is for me and all kings to read."

This wasn't, however, the starting-point of Henry's alienation from the papacy. That was due not so much to political theory as to his personal problem. At the beginning of his reign Henry had married Catherine of Aragon, daughter of the King of Spain, with a due dispensation by the Pope from the bond of her previous marriage to Henry's elder brother Arthur, who had died shortly afterwards. At first, all went well, and Catherine was a popular Queen among the English. After a time, however, Henry came to be attracted to one of her handmaids, Anne Boleyn, niece to the powerful Duke of Norfolk, as much for her remarkable wit as for her beauty. A devotee of the mediaeval ideal of chivalry, as depicted from the beginning of the Tudor period in Sir Thomas Malory's *Morte Darthur* (printed by Caxton in 1485), Henry regarded her as his mistress and wrote her a series of ardent love letters which are still preserved in the Vatican Museum. But she was unwilling to be merely mistress. She insisted on being Henry's Queen. Thus the matter passed from the personal to the political realm, and from being a merely domestic problem it became an affair of national importance, or what More called "the King's great matter".

Nor was this merely a matter of romantic attachment on the

King's part, for which he desired a divorce from his Queen. Despite his royal power, he needed legal justification for his desire. For this he claimed the authority of the Bible, as proposed in the Book of Leviticus, both Lev. xviii.16, "Thou shalt not uncover the nakedness of thy brother's wife," and Lev. xx.21, "If a man take his brother's wife, it is an unclean thing . . . they shall be childless." In fact, Catherine had been wife to Henry's brother Arthur, and since the death of Arthur and her remarriage to Henry she had failed to give him the male offspring he expected, though she hadn't been altogether childless. This was, however, enough for the King to entertain religious doubts about the validity of the papal dispensation which had been granted him and her at the time of their marriage. Accordingly, from 1526 onwards he chose to live apart from the Queen till such time as his doubts might be resolved. The following year a formal inquiry was instituted by Cardinal Wolsey, Archbishop of York, and Archbishop Warham of Canterbury, and before them Catherine denied that there had been any consummation of her marriage with Arthur, who had fallen ill at the same time. The Pope, therefore, appointed a commission to deal with the matter in 1528, this time under Cardinal Wolsey and Cardinal Campeggio as his legates, but on the one occasion Catherine appeared before the court, she appealed to Rome and her case had to be referred to a Roman court.

Henry, however, considered it beneath his royal dignity to appear before a court at Rome on such a personal matter. He held Wolsey to blame for his failure to bring the proceedings to a satisfactory conclusion, and so the latter was replaced as Chancellor by More in 1529. The large place of Wolsey was occupied not only by More but also by Wolsey's assistant Thomas Cromwell and by another new figure, Thomas Cranmer, who was soon to succeed Warham as Archbishop of Canterbury. Unlike More, these two men were sympathizers with Luther and set on a policy of religious reformation. It was Cranmer who, while a scholar at Cambridge, had suggested to Henry the plan of gaining opinions favourable to the royal divorce from various universities in Europe, while it was Cromwell who proposed the idea that once the King was head of the Church in England, as was his right, he might speedily obtain his desired divorce from the Queen.

Practical measures were soon taken towards the realization of this royal desire by the summoning of Parliament in 1529, subsequently known as "the Reformation Parliament". It was, ironically, opened by the new Chancellor, Sir Thomas More, but in spite of More, it proceeded to pass a series of acts designed by Thomas Cromwell to reduce the authority of the Pope in England. In particular, it brought pressure to bear on the higher clergy by accusing them of having offended against the old statute of Praemunire, which had restricted appeals to Rome – in their acceptance of Cardinal Wolsey as Papal Legate in 1518, though in doing so they had had the royal approval. In 1532 they made their formal submission to the King, recognizing him as Supreme Head of the Church in England "in so far as the law of Christ allows". This was followed by an act in restraint of appeals to Rome in 1533, rejecting all papal jurisdiction over England with special reference to matrimonial and other causes, an act that has been called "perhaps the most important statute of the sixteenth century". The immediate consequence of this act was the holding of a court at Dunstable in Kent, presided over by Archbishop Cranmer, at which Henry's marriage with Catherine was declared null and void. A week later Anne Boleyn was crowned Queen, and only three months after her coronation she gave birth to a baby daughter, Elizabeth. On the other hand, Henry was in turn excommunicated by Pope Clement VII in the same year, and his divorce and remarriage were declared null and void.

There followed two further acts of deep significance in 1534. First came the Act of Succession, ratifying Henry's secret marriage with Anne and entailing the crown on her children, while at the same time requiring all leading members of the realm to take an oath accepting both the divorce and the succession. Next came the Act of Supremacy, proclaiming Henry "the only supreme head in earth of the Church of England, called *Anglicana Ecclesia*", omitting the stipulated addition of "in so far as the law of Christ allows". More and Fisher, who refused to take the oath, were committed to the Tower of London – the former having already resigned his office of Chancellor in 1532, on finding his position increasingly difficult to maintain. In the following year the Act of Treason was passed, extending the definition of "treason" to any criticism of the King and refusal to admit his new claims. Thus the way was open to send first Fisher in June, then More in July, to their execution as "traitors" – though such a deed evoked a storm of protest throughout Europe.

Thus the religious reformation in England was initiated with due attention to the forms of law, as Parliament was directed and often impelled to that end by Thomas Cromwell, himself a lawyer. Till then the two powers, temporal and spiritual, had been kept theoretically separate between King and Pope (represented by the Archbishop of Canterbury), though in the twelfth century Henry II had tried to take over considerable power from the Church in face of opposition from the Archbishop, St Thomas à Becket. Now these powers were united for the first time in one ruler, Henry VIII, to the exclusion of papal authority. Yet the Church in England under Henry still maintained Catholic teaching and was still opposed to the teaching of Luther. On the other hand, behind Henry himself stood three powerful Lutheran sympathizers, not only Cromwell and Cranmer, but also the new Queen, Anne Boleyn.

Now, too, the King appointed Thomas Cromwell as vicar-general in ecclesiastical affairs in 1535, and at once Cromwell proceeded to set afoot a comprehensive visitation of all monasteries in the kingdom. He had already been employed by Wolsey in the task of suppressing certain lesser monasteries for the foundation of two colleges, one at Ipswich, Wolsey's home town, and the other at Oxford, and it was now his idea to extend this practice to strengthen the King's position while weakening that of the Church. The intended outcome of the visitation was an unfavourable report, based largely on scandal and hearsay, which the visitors encouraged the monks to tell them. This was the material used for a further Act of Parliament decreeing the dissolution of some 250 lesser monasteries in 1536. The act, or rather its execution, combined with fears of further such measures, evoked considerable protest in the remoter parts of the country, especially the counties of Lincoln and York, which came to a head in the Pilgrimage of Grace in October 1536. It was, however, put down by empty promises made by the Duke of Norfolk in the King's name and the leaders were then severely punished.

This was followed by the destruction of saints' shrines up and down the country in 1538, particularly the rich shrine of St Thomas of Canterbury, who was now held up as a traitor to his King, Henry II. Even the royal shrine of St Edward in Westminster Abbey suffered similar spoliation. Then it was the turn of the greater abbeys, such as Glastonbury and Bury St Edmunds, to be dissolved in 1539, and by the following year the work of destruction was completed. Thus in the six years following on the King's claim to be spiritual head of the Church in England, a large section of that Church was destroyed and its wealth confiscated by the King or granted to his courtiers for their support in all his religious changes. From some of the abbey churches, such as those at Bristol, Chester, Gloucester, Oxford and Peterborough, new dioceses were erected, but for the most part their wealth was used by the King for his own selfish purposes and for waging an unsuccessful but costly war against France.

Now everywhere in England one might behold what Shakespeare sadly mentions in one of his sonnets as "bare ruined choirs, where late the sweet birds sang". For all the defects of the former monks, as indicated even by Sir Thomas More in his *Utopia*, there can be no doubt that the dissolution of the monasteries was a serious setback to the causes of charity and education, considering how the monks had traditionally cared for the poor and provided education for children. With the monastic buildings, moreover, much priceless ecclesiastical art was destroyed, together with many manuscripts from the monastic libraries – much to the horror of humanists, who saw England as lapsing into a new barbarism. As for the poor, it is from now onwards that we come upon a series of statutes dealing with the alarming increase of those named as "rogues, vagabonds and sturdy beggars". The monastic property didn't long remain in the hands of the King or his courtiers who received or purchased it from him. Much of it came to pass from one owner to another, causing those who lived on the land to be increasingly afflicted with insecurity. In short, the whole realm might be described in the words of Shakespeare's riddling gardener in *Richard II* as "full of weeds, her fairest flowers choked up, / Her fruit-trees all unpruned, her hedges ruined, / Her knots disordered, and her wholesome herbs / Swarming with caterpillars" (iii.4).

Finally, by way of epilogue, it may be of interest to note the fate of the principal architects of this sad state of affairs. First, Anne Boleyn, for whom all these changes had been made that she might enjoy the dignity of Queen, didn't long enjoy the King's favour. In 1536 she was charged with infidelity to her husband, involving sexual intercourse with several persons, condemned to death and beheaded in the Tower of London. Secondly, Thomas Cromwell, who had stage-managed the whole course of the Reformation in England, at last overreached himself by planning the fourth royal marriage with a Lutheran princess, Anne of Cleves, in 1540. That year he was created Earl of Essex, but before the year was out, when the King found the princess not to his liking, the new earl found himself accused by his enemies of treason and beheaded. As for Henry himself, he died in 1547 of a repulsive disease, after having been divorced from two of his queens, beheaded two others, and lost one in childbirth.

In the following reign of the boy-King Edward VI, only Thomas Cranmer survived to become the leading figure in the Protestant Reformation that was from now on effected in England. He not only invited leading Protestant reformers, Peter Martyr and Martin Bucer, to come and spread their teaching at the two universities of Oxford and Cambridge, but he was also largely instrumental in translating and adapting the new English liturgy, of which further mention will be made in the next chapter. After six years of Protestant domination under Edward VI, however, Cranmer had to submit to the Catholic rule of Edward's half-sister Mary. He was then charged with treason but was spared, though in the event he was unable to escape the further charge of heresy, for which he was burnt at the stake at Oxford with two "episcopal" companions in March 1556.

Among the above-mentioned personalities who figured in the English Reformation under Henry VIII – many of them named Thomas! – it is paradoxically only Sir Thomas More who stands out as blessed. He may have been executed by the King in 1536 on the charge of treason, but for this very reason he stands out as a martyr for the sake of conscience and human rights, as well as for the Catholic Church. He may thus be regarded as a champion of humanity against the new power of royal absolutism, and as such he became the subject of many biographies in his own century, till today he is hailed, in the words of his friend Erasmus, as "a man for all seasons".

Chapter 2

THE LITURGICAL ISSUE
LATIN VS ENGLISH

Even in limiting one's attention to the Reformation within England, it is necessary to turn again and again to Luther as the mainspring and source of Protestantism. His appeal to the people of his time was not only religious but also nationalistic. That nationalism of his, moreover, appeared not only in his addresses to the German princes and people against what seemed to many the domination of the Church by Italians, but also in his effective use of the German tongue. In such a situation it was natural for him to proceed to a translation of the Bible into the German language as well as an adaptation of the liturgy in the same tongue. In this way his name has come to stand at the beginning of a new German literature.

Up till his time, at least in the West, the unity of the Church was widely seen as bound up with the use of the common liturgical language, Latin. With the decline of the Roman Empire, the Latin language, too, had come to decline and to reappear in the variety of so-called Romance languages – Italian, Spanish, Provençal and French – while variously influencing the different languages of the Germanic lands beyond the ancient boundaries of the Empire. At the same time, the old "vulgate", or common, Latin of St Jerome and St Augustine remained the standard of mediaeval Latin, though with the passing of the years it became increasingly fixed and rigid. Then its power to unify the countries of Christendom came to be undermined by the rise of nationalism and the growth of national languages and literatures.

In Luther, therefore, one may see the clash of the new movement against the old tradition, the national spirit of self-assertion against the old concern for the unity of Christendom. This clash one finds crystallized in his great task of translating the Bible into German, not from the Latin Vulgate of St Jerome, but from the original Hebrew of the Old Testament and the original Greek of the New Testament. This task he began during his period of seclusion in the Wartburg Castle under the necessary protection of Frederick the Elector of Saxony, and this resulted in his publication of the German New Testament in 1522, though his Old Testament didn't attain completion till 1534.

In this task Luther's principal aim wasn't merely linguistic or literary, as it were responding to the famous wish of Erasmus expressed in the preface to his edition of the Greek New Testament (or *Novum Instrumentum*) in 1516, "I wish that even the weakest woman should read the Gospels and the Epistles of St Paul. And I wish these were translated into all languages. . . . I long that the husbandman should sing portions of them to himself as he follows the plough, that the weaver should hum them to the tune of the shuttle, that the traveller should beguile with their stories the tedium of his journey." Rather, there was a deep theological implication in the task, namely that of vindicating his teaching on faith in the Word of God instead of what he regarded as the merely human tradition of the Church. This was the characteristic of all his teaching, to set conflicting principles at odds with each other and to reject any form of reconciliation as compromise – Faith against Works, the Word of God against the words of men, the Bible against the Church, Scripture against Tradition, and private judgment against ecclesiastical authority. He made his appeal at once to nationalism and individualism, in the name of freedom, against the authority of the universal Church with its concern for unity and tradition.

Turning back from Germany to England, one notes a steady increase among Luther's followers. The leading place among these followers soon came to be occupied by William Tyndale, who had also been inspired by Erasmus to undertake the task of translating the Bible into English. Finding no encouragement from the English bishops, he made his way to Germany, where he came under the influence of Luther. By 1525 he had completed his translation of the New Testament, which was printed partly at Cologne, partly at Worms. The effect of this translation on the Lutheran movement in England was considerable, and in its long-term effects it is seen as entering into subsequent Tudor translations of the Bible, culminating in the Authorized Version of 1611. In the religious controversies of the time from now onwards its power as a weapon on the Lutheran side was recognized by Sir Thomas More in his writings against Tyndale from 1528, in the use of such words as "congregation" in place of "church", "senior" or "elder" in place of "priest", "favour" in place of "grace", "knowledge" in place of "confession", and "repentance" in place of "penance". In using such words Tyndale suggests a novel Protestant interpretation instead of the traditional Catholic interpretation of Scripture.

At this point it may be asked why the Church was so reluctant to allow vernacular translations of the Bible at this time. For one thing, as More pointed out, the Latin Vulgate of St Jerome was considered sufficient for the reading of learned men, whose responsibility was to explain the "strong meat" of Scripture in the simpler, easier form of "milk for babes" to the common people. After all, in the Bible there was much that lent itself to misinterpretation by individuals to their own undoing, as St Peter himself warned his readers in II Peter iii.16. Some parts might well be accepted in their simple, literal sense, but others had to be interpreted in a deeper, spiritual sense, according to the traditional teaching of the Fathers. For another, once Luther's ideas had begun to spread in Europe, the translation of the Bible into the vernacular language came to be regarded as the rallying cry of heretics, and so the reaction of ecclesiastical authorities was understandably cautious and negative. This, however, only made it seem as if the Bible was on the side of the new teaching.

As for Henry VIII, even when he came to be recognized as Supreme Head of the Church in England, he refused to admit the new ideas of Luther or Tyndale, and his agents were largely responsible for bringing the latter to his burning for heresy in 1536. To the end of his reign he maintained the old liturgy in

Latin, regarding himself as the true defender of the Catholic faith in his kingdom. All the same, he was encouraged by Cranmer and Cromwell to sponsor the translation of the Bible into English. Already in 1534 the convocation of the Church at Canterbury submitted a petition to the King for permission to translate the whole Bible into English, though this wasn't immediately granted. Yet in the following year the first complete Bible in English translation was published by Miles Coverdale and dedicated to the King, though without his official approval. This was based, wherever possible, on Tyndale's translation, and the many gaps in the latter were supplied from Luther's German owing to Coverdale's insufficient knowledge of Hebrew. A revised version named "Matthew's Bible", edited by the Lutheran John Rogers, was the first to be authorized by the King in 1537, but its many notes with a Protestant bias made it unsuitable for official use. This was why a further revision of Tyndale and Coverdale without notes was provided by the Great Bible, which was published in 1539 under the patronage of Cromwell. Then on the latter's fall from grace in 1540, a new edition was published with a preface by Cranmer. In this form the Bible was ordered to be placed in churches throughout the realm so that all the King's subjects might freely read it for themselves.

As for the translation of the liturgy into English, this was a more delicate matter, involving as it did a radical change in the religious worship of the common people. It was therefore not effected during the reign of Henry VIII, whose Catholic sympathies were fostered by Stephen Gardiner, Bishop of Winchester, after the death of Cromwell. But when Henry was succeeded in 1547 by the boy-King Edward VI, whose sympathies were Protestant, Cranmer and his friends found themselves free to follow their Lutheran tendencies and to invite German reformers to come and spread their teachings in England. In particular, Cranmer, as Archbishop of Canterbury, was commissioned to draw up a new English liturgy, which was printed under the title of *The Book of Common Prayer* and authorized for use in all churches by the Act of Uniformity in 1549. As such, it represented a compromise between traditional Catholics and radical Protestants, retaining as it did the use of vestments, prayers for the dead, and the Catholic theology of sacrifice. Owing to strong Protestant criticism, however, it was reformulated in 1552 in a second *Book of Common Prayer*, which provided for the use of a surplice without other vestments and omitted all reference to the Mass and the altar. Its authorization was, however, forestalled by the death of Edward VI and the accession of his Catholic half-sister Mary in 1553. Only when Elizabeth I came to the throne on the death of Mary in 1558 was this second Book ratified in a new Act of Uniformity, if with a few minor alterations, and took effect throughout the realm.

This *Book of Common Prayer* in both its versions was mainly the work of Cranmer himself, and its style is characterized by his stately English prose, which has exercised a profound influence on the mindset of the Church of England. No one attending the traditional Anglican services, particularly the Communion service, from childhood onwards, can escape the peculiar quality of this style and the mind of Cranmer implicit in it. At the same time, it subtly conveys his theological ideas on the sacrament of the Eucharist, according to which the Catholic Mass is regarded no longer as a sacrifice renewed in place and time but as no more than a commemoration of the Lord's Supper. For him the sacrificial and sacramental aspects of the Mass were of subordinate importance to the reading of Holy Scripture, concerning which he also composed one of the homilies that were issued towards the end of Henry's reign and reissued with a second volume early on in the reign of Elizabeth. On this point he contrasted "the well of life" to be found in Holy Scripture with "the stinking puddles" of ecclesiastical tradition, adding: "Nothing more darkeneth (the mind) than doth the ignorance of God's word."

In this attitude of Cranmer one may notice a characteristic of the English Reformation as contrasted with that of Luther in Germany. In England the emphasis wasn't so much theoretical or theological as practical and liturgical, with an insistence that both the Bible and the liturgy should be in a language intelligible to ordinary people. As Cranmer put it in his preface to the *Book of*

Common Prayer, "Here is ordained nothing to be read but the very pure word of God, the holy scriptures, or that which is evidently grounded upon the same, and that in such a language and order as is most easy and plain for the understanding both of the readers and hearers." This is what one finds both in the early controversy between More and Tyndale in the reign of Henry VIII, where the main issue seems to be that of translation, and in the subsequent "great controversy" between Jewel and Harding in the first decade of Elizabeth's reign, where the main issue was that of the sacrifice of the Mass.

Finally, turning to Elizabeth's reign, it is necessary to pay attention not just to the re-enactment of the second *Book of Common Prayer* (with minor alterations) in the Parliament of 1559, but also to further translations of the Bible, of which a need was still felt. Already the translations published in the reign of Henry VIII had come to seem old-fashioned, if only in the matters of spelling and black-letter typing. During the sixties, therefore, two new translations appeared, which remained the dominant versions till they were superseded by the King James or "Authorized" Version of 1611.

The first of these was the Geneva version in 1560, brought out under Puritan auspices and the editorship of William Whittingham, one of the Protestant exiles in Geneva during the reign of Mary. It was published in ordinary type, in a convenient, handy size, with marginal notes in a Calvinist sense, and it was the first English Bible to number the verses in each chapter. It became the version most widely used by people in Elizabethan England, whether Puritans or otherwise. Later in 1568 the Bishops' Bible was published as the official version for use in churches. It was for the most part a revision of the Great Bible and, like the latter, it refrained from the addition of notes. Its impact on the English mind was chiefly because of its use in the liturgy, while the Psalms were taken from the *Book of Common Prayer* according to the older version of the Great Bible.

It is, moreover, interesting to note the impact of both versions on the plays of Shakespeare, as shown in Richmond Noble's authoritative study *Shakespeare's Biblical Knowledge* (1935). Of the two versions, Noble remarks, there is a more recognizable influence of the Bishops' Bible on the earlier plays, as if reflecting the impression made on the dramatist's mind by his hearing of passages from the Bible read out in church, whereas in the later plays from *Hamlet* onwards there is a stronger influence of the Geneva Bible, as if reflecting the personal reading of the dramatist. Not that this impact need be taken as evidence of a Protestant tendency in the dramatist's mind, considering how difficult it was for him to have access to the one Catholic translation of the New Testament, which was published in 1582. Rather, it shows his readiness to draw profit as well from biblical translation as from mediaeval tradition both for the language of his plays and for the view of human life implicit in them. On the one hand, he seems to lament the destruction of those "bare ruined choirs, where late the sweet birds sang", while on the other, he willingly avails himself of the linguistic and literary riches brought to him by the translators of the English Bible, which may be said to have undergone in his plays what he calls in *The Tempest* "a sea-change / into something rich and strange".

Chapter 3

THE DOCTRINAL ISSUE
CATHOLIC VS PROTESTANT

In speaking of the sixteenth-century Reformation, even when we limit our reference to England, we have to recognize that the main issue was neither merely political nor liturgical but doctrinal. It is also significant that this movement occurred in an age both of growing nationalism, as we see in Germany and England, and of individualistic self-assertion, as we see in Martin Luther and Henry VIII. It is no less significant that it occurred at a time when a new vernacular literature was coming to birth in those nations, and it was only to be expected that this literature should have its fine flower in the translation not only of the Bible but also of the liturgy. These issues are prominent in the early stages of the Reformation in England, first when Henry VIII presented himself as Supreme Head of the Church in England, and then when the translation of the Bible into English was followed up in the reign of Edward VI in the form of two successive *Books of Common Prayer*. Gradually, however, the more fundamental doctrinal issue comes to the fore, particularly during the early years of Elizabeth's reign, reflecting a new interpretation of Christianity arising out of a new reading of the Bible and resulting in a new opposition to Catholic tradition which came to be known as "Protestant" from the formal protest of the reforming party presented at the Diet of Speyer in 1529.

This basic issue goes back to the original position of Luther in his new, personal interpretation of the Bible. Basic to this position is his thesis that the sole source of divine revelation and the sole authority for Christian faith is the Bible as being the word of God.

It is in consequence of this thesis that the Bible is set against the Church, which is by contrast seen as a merely human institution, adding human traditions as glosses to the divine word. In this approach to the text of the Bible, moreover, particular insistence is laid on its plain, literal meaning as opposed to the figurative, allegorical or spiritual meanings which had come in the course of time to overlay the literal meaning, according to the teachings of Origen and St Augustine. Not that the Church, which already appears in the pages of the New Testament, is altogether rejected, but it is explained as the spiritual, invisible, ideal Church, revealed in the concluding vision of the Apocalypse, in contrast to the visible Church on earth, which is all too subject to human defects and abuses. In this rejection of the visible Church there appears what Catholics saw as the characteristic heresy of Luther, especially when he went on to call into question the hierarchical order of the Church and the seven sacraments, admitting only those of baptism and communion as instituted by Christ himself.

Even more basic than this general emphasis on the Bible as opposed to the Church in Luther's reforming vision is his answer to the question of man's salvation as he found it in the two epistles of St Paul to the Romans and the Galatians. In particular, he took his stand on St Paul's assertion of justification by Faith in Christ, as opposed to the Pharisaic insistence on the Works of the law – where St Paul (in Rom. i.17) is in turn quoting the words of the prophet Habacuc, "The just man lives by faith" (Hab. ii.4). In taking this stand, Luther was guided by his own personal experience, on finding how difficult it was for him to live according to his religious rule in all its details. But then, on reading these words of St Paul, he was struck as it were by light from heaven or, as C S Lewis puts it, quoting the sonnet of William Wordsworth, "surprised by joy". So deep was his confidence in this enlightenment of his spirit, that he was able to maintain it in the face of the combined opposition of the Church and the Empire at the Diet of Worms in 1521. Then he is said to have stated, "*Ich kann nicht anders*", which might be rendered in Chaucer's English as "I can no more."

In other words, what is basic to Luther's teaching is that

faith in Jesus Christ which he professed to have found in the epistles of St Paul. This isn't merely an intellectual assent to the creed, but rather a confidence in Jesus Christ as Saviour, with an accompanying refusal to put any trust in one's good works as in any way contributing to one's salvation. Such good works may have their place in this world for the fostering of good relations among human beings on earth, but their only value in the sight of God is the extent to which they are inspired by faith in Jesus Christ. Thus in addition to the opposition drawn by Luther between the Bible and the Church, Scripture and Tradition, the invisible and the visible Church, there is this further opposition between Faith and Works, which is comparable to that between Grace and Nature, or the spirit and the flesh. In its extreme form it was stated in other words of Luther to Philip of Hesse on the subject of adultery, "*Pecca fortiter, sed crede fortius!*" – "Sin strongly, but believe all the more strongly" – words which he reiterated on more than one occasion. It was particularly for such teaching that he came to be criticized by Catholic writers of the age, such as Thomas Harding in his *Answer* to John Jewel, for "the carnal liberty of this new gospel". It is also what we find subsequently echoed by two of Shakespeare's riotous characters, Sir John Falstaff and Sir Toby Belch.

What Luther went on to affirm is that this faith is entirely the work of God and the free gift of his mercy, without any merit on the part of human beings, who are all deserving of damnation as much for the original sin of Adam as for their own actual sins. It is what Hamlet, who has been studying at Wittenberg, says to Polonius, "Use every man after his desert, and who should 'scape whipping?" (ii.2) and what he later says to Ophelia, "We are arrant knaves, all. Believe none of us!" (iii.1). This faith may serve to justify and so save the sinner, but it none the less leaves him in his sins, since the grace of God is, according to Luther, merely "imputed" to man without basically altering his sinful nature. In Luther's eyes human nature is utterly corrupted by sin, and so the human will is deprived of the freedom to do good in the sight of God. It is only the mercy of God that bestows grace on human beings in view of the merits of Jesus Christ, while they themselves remain without anything of which they can boast. It thus seems that Luther's teaching is basically pessimistic about human nature, with a pessimism that is directly contrary to the optimism of the Renaissance humanists. On this point, therefore, it isn't surprising that the humanist Erasmus, though originally sympathetic to Luther's biblical viewpoint, came out against him with his characteristic *De Libero Arbitrio* (1524), to which Luther no less characteristically responded with his *De Servo Arbitrio* (1525). In Luther's view, however, this pessimism merely served to set forth in bolder relief his Christian optimism and joy in Christ who had freed him from slavery to the works of the law.

Turning now from Germany to England, it is true that the origin of the English Reformation is to be seen in the personal desires of Henry VIII and his consequent determination to establish his independence from the authority of Rome in the pursuit of those desires. Yet till the end he regarded himself as Catholic, a defender of the orthodox faith and a persecutor of heresy. It is also true that much of the impulse of the English reformers is to be seen in their desire to have the Bible and the liturgy translated into their own English tongue, as Luther had done for Germany. But with the death of Henry VIII and the accession of Edward VI, followed at an interval by Elizabeth I, the new teaching of the Protestant reformers was allowed full freedom to spread in England, while the traditional Catholic teaching was denied any such freedom. From then onwards, not only the original vision of Luther but also that of successive reformers, particularly that of the Swiss Zwingli at Zurich and the French Calvin at Geneva, came to be promulgated with official approval throughout the land. This was, moreover, effected under the supervision of the new Elizabethan bishops who were all Protestant, replacing Mary's bishops, who now remained firm – unlike Henry's bishops – in their assertion of "the old faith".

The doctrinal issue now appears in the first major controversy of Elizabeth's reign, that which took place during the 1560s between the Catholic theologian Thomas Harding, from his land of exile in Louvain, and the Anglican bishop of Salisbury, John Jewel. Concerning this controversy, which is ignored in most discussions of Elizabethan history and literature, one may quote the admiring comment of Shakespeare's contemporary, Dr Gabriel Harvey of Cambridge University, looking back on it over a gap of some thirty years: "Harding and Jewel were our Aeschines and Demosthenes, and scarcely any language in the Christian world hath afforded a pair of adversaries equivalent to Harding and Jewel, two thundering and lightning orators in divinity" (from his *Pierces Supererogation*, 1593).

This all began with the challenge issued by Jewel in a sermon he repeated three times at the beginning of the new reign, in late 1559 and early 1560. He opened with the vaunting words quoted above as characteristic of the new reformed teaching, "It hath pleased almighty God of his great mercy in these our days to remove away all such deformities and to restore again the same holy mysteries to the first original . . . forasmuch as the glorious light of the Gospel of Christ is now so mightily spread abroad." From these general words Jewel went on to lay down an explicit challenge concerning such points of contention with Catholics as the real presence, adoration of the blessed sacrament, transubstantiation, the veneration of images, the use of Latin for Mass, and the custom of saying Mass in private, even sometimes on the same day in the same church. "If any learned man of all our adversaries," he exclaimed, "or if all the learned men that be alive, be able to bring any one sufficient sentence out of any old Catholic doctor or father, or out of any old general council, or out of the holy scriptures of God . . . I would give over and subscribe unto him."

The first Catholic theologian to take up this challenge was the Marian Dean of St Paul's, Dr Henry Cole, who was however restricted by his situation in confinement and by his undertaking not to engage in open disputation. He therefore wrote a private letter of protest to Jewel, demanding why his adversary offers to dispute on such minor points rather than on "the chief matters that lie in question betwixt the Church of Rome and the Protestants". Then he went on to make the claim, "We continue in the faith we professed sith our baptism, ye pretend a change in the same. We have with us an apostolical church, ye have none yet approved. We make no innovation. . . . We are in possession, ye come to put us from it." Immediately he was taken up and answered by Jewel in a series of letters that were soon published, with the last word on the Anglican side. Thus to Cole's claim Jewel replied, in his characteristically taunting manner, "He that will make any innovation, say you, must give a reason of his doings. O master doctor, this reason fighteth most against yourself. For you have misliked and put away the most part of the order of the primitive Church, and yet never gave any good reason of your doings." In brief, it was from the outset the Anglican contention that "our doctrine is old", going back to the time of Christ and his apostles, whereas "yours is new", having been introduced at some unspecified time since the age of the Fathers.

This controversy was, however, taken up more at length and with greater freedom by Thomas Harding, once he and his fellow-exiles had had time to settle down in the Low Countries, at the University of Louvain, and could set up a printing-press there. Now in his *Answer to Jewel's Challenge*, published in 1564, Harding returned to the same point at which Cole had begun his criticism. "Thus craftily," he insinuates, "you shift your hands off those greater points . . . and cast unto us, as a bone to gnaw upon, this number of articles of less weight, a few excepted, to occupy us withal, which be partly concerning order rather than doctrine." He also went on to accuse Jewel of innovation in having "set up a religion of your own forging, a new church of your own framing, a new gospel of your own device." For the most part he dwelt on the Catholic theology of the Mass, as being the most basic of the articles offered by Jewel for disputation. Like Thomas More in his earlier dispute with William Tyndale, he took particular exception to his opponent's use of unaccustomed theological and liturgical terms. "By the word 'sign', he notes, "he meaneth the sacrament, liking better that strange word than the accustomed word of the Church. . . . He dissembleth the word of the sacrifice (*divinam oblationem*) . . . and termeth it otherwise in his replies by the name of 'common prayers' . . . refusing the word of the Church."

This *Answer*, however, didn't long remain unanswered by Jewel, who now came out with a *Reply* to Harding in the following year. In it Jewel explained his reason for refusing to use the customary words of the Church. "We appeal," he declares, "from the Church to Christ, from the party to the judge, from the Church deformed to the Church reformed, from a Church particular to the Church catholic, from the false to the true, from the new to the old, from a doubtful, variable, uncertain, unadvised sentence to a sentence most firm, most stable, most certain, most constant, that shall stand firm forever." Then on his side Harding published a *Rejoinder* in 1566, emphasizing Christ's promise of his abiding presence in his Church, though this is ignored by the would-be reformers. "These fellows," he says, "would have us believe that after six hundred years Christ waxed weary of his spouse the Church, as some men be of their old wives, and was divorced from her." On the other hand, he defied the reformers to show any evidence "of such antiquity, of such order of succession, of so long continuance, of so large spreading over the world in any of your congregations."

At the same time, these two champions became engaged in another, wider ranging controversy arising out of Jewel's brief *Apology for the Church of England*, which was published first in Latin in 1562, so as to be read by a wider educated public overseas, but soon translated into English. Here it was Jewel's aim to justify the seeming sin of schism in the separation of England from the unity of the Catholic Church. "As touching what we have now done," he pleaded, the Anglicans have departed "from that Church whose errors were proved and made manifest to the world." Or rather, they have departed "not so much from itself as from the errors thereof," and that "not disorderly or wickedly but quietly and soberly," in such a way as to do nothing "against the doctrine either of Christ or of his apostles." Therefore he maintains, "We have called home again to the original and first foundation that religion which hath been foully foreslowed and utterly corrupted by these men . . . forasmuch as we heard God himself speaking to us in his word." In response, Harding came out with his most representative *Confutation* of 1565, in the course of which he has the following fierce words of indignation in defence of the old faith, "The Church hath not erred, nor lacked the Holy Ghost, the Spirit of truth, these nine hundred years past, according to Christ's promise. . . . The practice of the gospellers is utterly to set the Church at naught and with a hot raging spirit to defy it, and to say that themselves be the Catholic Church, and that the Catholics be the Papistical Church, the Church of Antichrist, the whore of Babylon, a den of thieves, and I cannot tell what. . . . It standeth not with Christ's promises . . . that he should suffer his Church to continue in darkness and lack of truth these thousand years past, and now at the latter days to reveal the truth of his gospel by apostates, vow-breakers, church-robbers and such other most unlike to the apostles."

Thus we find in this further controversy, and in related controversies that now sprang up on either side of the English Channel, a widening of the doctrinal issue from the more practical or liturgical one of the Mass to the more general one of the true Church of Christ. On this issue it was the Anglican contention that true antiquity was on their side, in view of the doctrinal corruptions that had crept into the mediaeval Church, whereas the Catholics maintained that the promise of Christ to his Church was no less valid in the past than in the present, in opposition to the novel teaching of Luther and his followers. In all this discussion, however, less attention was paid – on account of the terms initially proposed by Jewel – to the basic question of human corruption by sin and justification by grace. Rather, the English approach to the matter may be seen as of a more practical and even mystical nature, with emphasis on the question, subsequently echoed by the poet John Donne in one of his divine poems, "Where is the true Church of Christ?"

This was merely the beginning of a long series of controversies which, so far from abating, only grew in intensity and variety throughout the reign of Elizabeth I and well into that of James I and Charles I. If a particular controversy came to an end, it wasn't because one side was considered to have won the victory, or because of weariness on the other side, but because in each case it was one side, the Anglican, who had the upper hand by wielding not the pen but the sword. This was the continual complaint of the Catholics in particular, that the Anglicans were free to offer as many challenges as they liked, but that the Catholics weren't free to take up those offers. Or if they took up those offers in their land of exile, they could only smuggle their books into England under various penalties that in time came to involve the death penalty. Then, when the Catholics were for a time silenced and turned their attention to the more practical need of providing priests for their persecuted countrymen by means of the seminary at Douai, founded in 1568, further controversies broke out between the Anglicans and the more radical Puritans. Then, ironically, the former found themselves in the position of defending that Catholic tradition which had come down to them in England through the ages of the old faith, against Puritan accusations of "new Popery".

In consequence of all these controversies, to the right and to the left, there developed an atmosphere of intellectual and religious debate which called in question the most fundamental articles of the faith. Such precisely was the atmosphere in which the Elizabethan drama came to flourish in the course of the reign, though all open discussion of religious and political questions was strictly forbidden. At the same time, the controversy didn't remain for long on the high level of academic or doctrinal debate, but soon, with the increasing readiness of the Anglicans to fall back on the argument of the sword, it descended to the lower level of inquisition and persecution, notably against the more numerous Papists (as they were increasingly called), and then against the more vociferous Puritan minority.

Chapter 4

THE RELIGIOUS ISSUE
TRAITORS OR MARTYRS?

In turning to what for convenience' sake I call "the religious issue", the situation as it developed in England is no longer related, like the previous issues, to that of Germany, but it is altogether peculiar to Tudor England. From the moment Henry VIII assumed the role of Supreme Head of the Church of England, there arose an almost inextricable association of religion and politics according to which any form of dissent from the King's religious policy entailed a charge of treason with the threat of capital punishment. From the very year in which the Act of Treason was passed in 1535, there begins an impressive line of victims, from Sir Thomas More and Bishop John Fisher onwards. Under Edward VI, however, the number somewhat declined, and under Mary the many Protestants who suffered did so not as traitors but as heretics under earlier laws. Finally, when Elizabeth came to the throne in 1558, she professed (like Mary before her) a policy of toleration, but the Act of Uniformity, which was passed in the following year, required attendance at the new English services and forbade the celebration of the Latin Mass with severe penalties attached to disobedience. In practice, too, there was increasing discrimination against those who adhered in any way to the forms of the old religion.

With the passing of time, moreover, it became increasingly difficult to maintain even a semblance of religious toleration. England was now officially a Protestant country, supporting the Protestant cause in such neighbouring countries as Scotland, Holland and France. At the same time, she stood out in opposition not only to the Pope in Rome but also to the Catholic King in

Spain and the powerful Catholic party in France led by the Duke of Guise. For this reason many Catholics in England were led to seek assistance from Spain and the Duke of Guise, as well as the Pope, and by so doing they came to be regarded as at least potential traitors to their country, suffering not so much for religious as for political reasons.

For the first ten years of the new reign the situation didn't seem to be so serious. The Catholics still hoped for a change of heart in the Queen, or at least, if she died, they could look for the accession of another Catholic Queen, Mary Stuart, who was next in line of succession. Meanwhile, they were deprived of their leaders, who had been either imprisoned or driven into exile, and so they easily submitted to the new laws, requiring attendance at the new services, while doing their best to attend Mass in secret. The Pope, too, waited to see how matters would turn out, and Elizabeth encouraged him to do so, though without any intention of altering her religious policy. This situation was, however, changed when Mary Stuart, driven from her country by her Protestant opponents at the battle of Langside in 1568, sought refuge with her royal cousin in England. The following year there took place the rising of the Northern earls, in support partly of Mary, partly of the Catholic cause, and this led the new Pope Pius V to issue his Bull of Excommunication against Elizabeth in 1570. Only by the time the bull reached England the rising had petered out, and vindictive measures were taken not only against the rebels but against the Catholics in general, who could now be shown up more than ever before as traitors.

It was about this time that a new breed of Catholic priests, who had been trained at the new seminary at Douai (shortly to be transferred to Rheims in France), began to return to England. They encouraged the Catholics to be more determined in their refusal to attend the Anglican services, but this only led the government to take stricter measures against them. From this time onwards, moreover, there appears a series of conspiracies against the Queen and her government, most of which were in fact devised by the government to cast discredit on the Catholics and to show them up as traitors. It was also from this time that a spy system was inaugurated by Sir William Cecil and his able assistant Sir Francis Walsingham to gather intelligence about the persons and movements of English Catholics both at home and abroad. Towards the end of the 1570s the Pope was persuaded to send a military expedition to Ireland, to assist the Irish Catholics in their resistance to the religious changes, but it also ended in failure. Though small in scale, it was sufficiently large to convince English Protestants that their Catholic countrymen were little better than traitors.

Such was the situation when the first Jesuits, notably Robert Persons and Edmund Campion, arrived in England in 1580. Their coming made more of an impression than that of the previous seminary priests in the mid-1570s, partly because of the more serious political situation, and partly because the Jesuits were more readily welcomed by the lay Catholics as spiritual leaders in view of their intellectual formation. From the outset a vigorous propaganda campaign was launched against them, and the ports were warned to be on the watch for them, but they succeeded in eluding the vigilance of the authorities and entering the country in disguise. Nor was it long before a new controversy broke out in which it was for once the Catholic side that went on the offensive with challenges issued by Campion against his Anglican opponents, defying them to engage in public disputation.

First, it was Persons who had to deal with the practical problem faced by Catholics as to whether they might not attend the Anglican services in view of the penalties attached to non-attendance. This he answered in the negative in a book published from a secret printing press in 1580 under the title of *A Brief Discourse Containing Certain Reasons why Catholics Refuse to go to Church*. In his preface under the assumed name of John Howlet, Persons made his appeal to the Queen herself, drawing her attention to the pitiful condition of her Catholic subjects who, "being now afflicted for their consciences and brought to such extremity as never was heard of in England before, have no other means to redress and ease their miseries, but only as confident children to run unto the mercy and clemency of your highness their mother and born sovereign princess, before whom, as before the substitute and angel of God, they lay down their griefs, disclose their miseries and unfold their pitiful afflicted case, brought into such distress at this time as either they must renounce God by doing that which in judgment and conscience they do condemn, or else sustain such intolerable molestations as they cannot bear." In the same preface Persons also gave detailed instances of the extreme penalties laid upon the practice of the Catholic religion as "imprisonment perpetual, loss of goods and lands and life also for the refusal of an oath against my religion, death for reconciling myself to God by my ghostly father, death for giving the supreme Pastor supreme authority in causes of the Church, death for bringing in a crucifix in remembrance of the Crucified, death for bringing in a silly pair of beads, a medal or an Agnus Dei, in devotion of the Lamb that took away my sins." Almost at once this book was attacked by no fewer than three Puritan writers, encouraged by the English government (notably by Sir William Cecil), partly as a convenient means of distracting their attention from their criticism of the Anglican bishops. Thus William Fulke came out with *A Brief Confutation of a Popish Discourse*, John Field with *A Caveat for Parsons Howlet*, and Perceval Wiburn with *A Check or Reproof of M. Howlet's Untimely Screeching*, all in the same year, 1580.

As for Campion, shortly after his arrival in England he was persuaded to pen his famous challenge, known as "Campion's Brag", in the form of nine articles challenging his Anglican opponents to a public disputation. This he wrote in the form of a "Letter to the Lords of the Council", to be delivered to them in the case of his not unlikely arrest. In fact, even before his eventual arrest in the following year, it came to the attention of the authorities and was published with a refutation by two Protestant ministers, also put up for this purpose by Cecil, William Charke with *An Answer to a Seditious Pamphlet* in 1580, and Meredith Hanmer with *The Great Brag and Challenge of M. Campion a Jesuit* in 1581. When Campion was arrested, his cause was taken up by his colleague Robert Persons, who published his *Brief Censure upon*

Two Books from the above-mentioned printing press in 1581. The tone of Campion's challenge may be gathered from the famous peroration of his letter. "Many innocent hands are lifted up to heaven for you daily by those English students, whose posterity shall never die, which beyond the seas, gathering virtue and sufficient knowledge for the purpose, are determined never to give you over, but either to win you heaven or to die upon your pikes. And touching our Society, be it known to you that we have made a league, all the Jesuits in the world, whose succession and multitude must overreach all the practices of England, cheerfully to carry the cross you shall lay upon us and never to despair your recovery, while we have a man left to enjoy your Tyburn or to be racked with your torments or consumed with your prisons. The expense is reckoned, the enterprise is begun. It is of God, it cannot be withstood. So the faith was planted, so it must be restored." On a more pedestrian level Persons went on to write *A Defence of the Censure* in 1582, in which he protested against the extreme vigilance of the English authorities making all disputation even in writing impossible. "You exclude us," he complained, "from speech, conference, writing, printing, disputing or any other due trial of our cause. You watch, spy, search, examine and persecute everywhere. You attach, drive away, put in prison, rent on rack, put to death those which speak or write or stand in defence of truth against you. You leave no inns, taverns, fields, stables, barns, dovecots, or palaces unsearched for us. And how then is it possible for us to answer you in writing?"

During the year before his arrest Campion also found the time to develop at greater length "ten reasons" for challenging the Anglican ministers to a disputation. These he set forth in the academic language of Latin under the title of *Rationes Decem*, which he had secretly printed and distributed in St Mary's church, Oxford in 1581. They caused a considerable sensation and provoked Latin responses, again orchestrated by Sir William Cecil, from the two Regius professors of divinity at the two universities, both of them prominent Puritans. At Cambridge William Whitaker brought out his *Ad Rationes Decem Edmundi Campiani Jesuitae* in

1581, and at Oxford Laurence Humphrey brought out his *Jesuitismi Pars Prima* in 1582, followed by the second part, *Jesuitismi Pars Secunda, seu Doctrinae Jesuiticae . . . Confutatio* in 1584.

Further, from the moment of his arrest and imprisonment in the Tower of London in the summer of 1581, other controversies of a more practical nature raged round Campion. First, by way of concession to his appeals for a disputation, a private conference was arranged between him and his Puritan opponents within the Tower. Only, whereas he was weakened by torture and denied access to books and other papers, his opponents came well supplied with books to support their arguments. Subsequently, in 1583 the proceedings were published under their auspices. Other writings at the time dealt with the various details of Campion's betrayal, arrest, imprisonment, tortures, trial and execution, from either side. A notable representative on the Protestant side was the pamphleteer and subsequent dramatist, Anthony Munday, who came out with his *Discovery of Edmund Campion* in 1582, while on the Catholic side an eye-witness account of the execution was provided by the seminary priest Thomas Alfield, in *A True Report of the Death and Martyrdom of M. Campion* also in 1582. The same year a fuller account was supplied by the president of the seminary, now at Rheims, William Allen, in his *Brief History of the Glorious Martyrdom of XII Reverend Priests*, with characteristic emphasis on the fact that, though they were sentenced to death as traitors, they died as martyrs or witnesses to the Catholic faith. It was above all out of this controversy that there appeared the widespread conviction among Catholics in both England and Europe that the situation in Elizabethan England amounted to a religious persecution, comparable to that endured by the Church in early Roman times. This conviction was chiefly fostered by Robert Persons with his Latin pamphlet, *De Persecutione Anglicana* in 1581, which was soon translated into both French and English the following year.

Meanwhile, from the side of the English government there came a series of pronouncements that justified the Catholics in their worst fears and prompted William Allen to speak out against them.

First, there were two royal proclamations, no doubt worded by Cecil himself, issued in July 1580 and again in January 1581, against the Jesuits and the seminary priests. They led Allen to publish his *Apology and True Declaration of the Institution and Endeavours of the Two English Colleges* (the one at Rheims and the other more recently founded at Rome) in 1581. Then, in view of the growing protest from royal courts in Europe against the barbarous use of torture in England, Cecil himself, now Lord Burghley, undertook to publish his *Declaration of the Favourable Dealing of Her Majesty's Commissioners appointed for the Examination of Certain Traitors* in 1583, followed by a fuller vindication of *The Execution of Justice in England*. Both these books were published in Latin translation in 1584. Against them Allen wrote his important vindication of the Catholic cause, possibly the most notable work of controversy on the Catholic side in this reign, under the title of *A True, Sincere and Modest Defence of English Catholics*, which came out in 1584. His main thesis was that the priests and others who suffered in the Catholic cause did so not as traitors but as martyrs. In particular, he repeated the previous complaint of Persons, which is abundantly vindicated by the evidence, that "most prisons in England be full at this day, and have been for divers years, of honourable and honest persons not to be touched with any treason or other offence in the world, other than their profession and faith in Christian religion." He also criticized the false fears aroused among the people against the Catholic danger, demanding, by contrast to the Catholic past of England, "Was there any such extreme fear of present invasion? Was there such mustering, such diligent watch and swearing against the Pope at every port, such examination of passengers, such ado generally, and such mistrust of the subjects' fidelity, such jealousy over all men, as though the whole realm were a camp?" It all sounds, one might note, like the situation evoked by Shakespeare at the beginning of *Hamlet*.

This dispute, as may well be seen, wasn't merely on the level of books but was carried on in close connection with deeds. On the one hand, the priests led by the Jesuits were becoming more daring and self-confident in their defence of the Catholic faith, for which they were ready to lay down even their lives. On the other hand, the authorities were more ready to resort to desperate measures, to the extent of employing all kinds of tortures and execution by the gruesome form of hanging, drawing and quartering the victim. From their point of view, as Claudius declares in *Hamlet*, "Diseases desperate grown / by desperate appliance are relieved, / or not at all" (iv.3). From now on these measures were even more intensely and frequently used, with more and more priests suffering the extreme penalty of death, while others languished in the various prisons of London and elsewhere, or else were more mercifully sent into exile. Also from now on a series of political events took place – the Babington Plot of 1586, supposedly for the rescue of Mary Stuart and the assassination of Elizabeth, the execution of Mary in 1587 for supposed complicity in that plot, and the sailing of the Spanish Armada in 1588, partly in revenge for Mary's execution – that seemed to justify the government in taking even more severe measures against the poor Catholics, till life for them become even more intolerable, with no end in sight.

All this, it may be added, is the immediate political and religious context for the appearance of the plays of William Shakespeare on the London stage from 1590 onwards. Accordingly, the natural question arising out of this context is what bearing it has on those plays, and how they fit into it, though this is a question which is all too rarely asked, considering how hardly the answer seems to come out of the plays.

Chapter 5

THE LITERARY ISSUE
IN SHAKESPEARE'S PLAYS

What connection, it must now be asked, is there between these various issues of the English Reformation – political, liturgical, doctrinal and religious – and the plays composed by Shakespeare towards the end of this tragic period? There is, of course, the negative connection, in that the Reformation brought to an end the religious drama of the Middle Ages, partly owing to the Puritan opposition to stage-plays as "popish", partly owing to the controversial use to which drama was being put early on in Elizabeth's reign, prompting her government to impose silence on the religious issue. It is in consequence of this measure that the drama of the Elizabethan age as a whole and of Shakespeare in particular is pervasively secular. There is also the indirect connection, in that the new translations of the Bible into English, encouraged by the Reformation, provided the dramatists of the age with a linguistic treasury on which Shakespeare drew more abundantly than any of his contemporaries.

This is why, when we turn from the religious controversies of the Tudor period to the plays of Shakespeare, we find ourselves as though entering into a different world, as though (to use Tennyson's words) "a door were shut between us and the sound". It seems to justify the attitude of those Shakespeare scholars who discuss the plays with little or no attention to their religious background. In any case, there seems to be so little in the plays which points in that direction. In this respect, there is such a contrast between the drama of Shakespeare, on the one hand, and the poetry of Spenser and Milton, on the other. Those two poets, the one patriotically

Protestant and the other more radically Puritan, are so obviously religious in all their writings, whereas if Shakespeare is religious, he seems to keep his religion very much to himself.

Turning now more specifically to the plays of Shakespeare, one feature which stands out in them all is the fact that they have their setting far from sixteenth-century England – till we come to his final history play of *Henry VIII*, which is now widely recognized as a work of collaboration with the younger Protestant dramatist for the King's Men, John Fletcher. In his romantic comedies Shakespeare looks away from his English home to the romantic lands of the Mediterranean, as it were finding there his cultural home – Ephesus, Verona, Padua, Navarre, Athens, Venice, Messina, the Ardennes, Illyria. Only in *The Merry Wives of Windsor* does he look up the River Thames to the town of Windsor as the setting for his play, at the special request of the Queen to see Falstaff in love. As for the plays of English history, he looks, as if with the eyes of Miranda in *The Tempest*, "in the dark backward and abysm of time" to the mediaeval past of England from the reign of King John till that of Richard III, but with the accession of Henry Tudor as Henry VII he falls silent. Even when at the end of his dramatic career he takes up the reign of Henry VIII, he is conspicuously silent on the religious issue of that reign, while concentrating on the personal and political issue of "the King's great matter". The tragedies, too, fall into the same pattern – either, like the comedies, looking to the lands of the Mediterranean, in Verona, Rome and Venice, or like the histories, looking back to the mediaeval past of Denmark and Scotland, or to the prehistoric past of Britain. It is as if in all these plays Shakespeare is doing his best to close his eyes to what is going on around him in Elizabethan England.

In these plays, moreover, the dramatist seemingly ignores the religious controversies in particular. Only by reading between the lines have scholars discerned indirect echoes and allusions that suggest his distaste at the way "sweet religion" is made a mere "rhapsody of words" (*Hamlet* iii.4) with all this endless disputation. Such, too, are the dying words of Mercutio in

Romeo and Juliet when, referring to the ceaseless strife between the Montagues and the Capulets, he calls down "a plague on both your houses" (iii.1) – especially when we consider the parallel in Shakespeare's England with the Catholic Montagues in Sussex and the Capels in neighbouring Hampshire. Such, more evidently, are the words of Helena in the contemporary *Midsummer Night's Dream*, protesting at the fight between Lysander and Demetrius as a "devilish-holy fray, when truth kills truth" (iii.2) – words that have a more obvious reference to the religious disputes of the time than to the immediate dramatic context. Such, too, are the words of Troilus when, in his disillusionment at the infidelity of Cressida, he feels that "the bonds of heaven are slipped, dissolved and loosed" (v.2). He goes on to comment, with as much reference to religious controversy as to his own state of mind, "O madness of discourse, that cause sets up with and against itself, bi-fold authority!" Above all, in *Measure for Measure* we at last have an explicit reference to religious controversy, in Lucio's gratuitous remark, "Grace is grace, despite of all controversy!" (i.2). His words stand out awkwardly from their dramatic context, but they apparently refer to the theological controversies on grace and free will which were then current both among the Anglicans (Calvinist against Arminian) in Cambridge and among the Catholics (Dominican against Jesuit) in Rome.

Of greater interest are the occasional references in the plays to the opposing parties in these disputes. To begin with, it may be noted that the term "Protestant", though current in English usage from the reign of Henry VIII, is never once used in the plays of Shakespeare. On the other hand, the derogatory epithet "Popish" is used once, in the early revenge play of *Titus Andronicus*, where it is put into the mouth of the villainous Aaron the Moor, when sneering at the conscientious Lucius, "Yet for I know thou art religious, / and hast a thing within thee called conscience, / with twenty popish tricks and ceremonies, / which I have seen thee careful to observe, / therefore I urge thy oath" (v.1). Again, the derogatory noun "Papist" is also used but once, in the later *All's Well That Ends Well*, where the clown Lavache refers slightingly to

"Old Poysam the Papist", only to be rebuked by the Countess as "a foul-mouthed and calumnious knave" (i.3). The term "Puritan", however, recurs more frequently in less favourable contexts. In the same scene of *All's Well* Lavache goes on to contrast the old Papist with "young Charbon the Puritan", referring no doubt to the fiery character of the radical Puritans in contrast to the more conservative Catholics. He also comments that "honesty is no Puritan", that is, not limited, as the Puritans liked to think, to members of their sect. Then in *Twelfth Night* the term is mentioned three times in one scene with derogatory reference to Malvolio, who has just disturbed Sir Toby and his friends in a drunken carousal. Maria remarks of him that "Sometimes he is a kind of Puritan", but she goes on to qualify her remark by saying, "The devil a Puritan that he is, or anything constantly, but a time-pleaser" (ii.3). In other words, Malvolio is presented not as a Puritan in the full, religious sense, but in its common contemporary usage as a self-satisfied hypocrite. Finally, among the last plays it is said of Marina in *Pericles*, that such is her chastity "she would make a Puritan of the devil" (iv.6), and in *The Winter's Tale* the other clown reports that among those at the sheep-shearing feast there is "but one Puritan amongst them, and he sings psalms to horn-pipes" (iv.2).

In general, comparing these various references to Papists and Puritans with each other, one gathers the impression that the dramatist is much more favourably disposed to the former than the latter. On the whole, however, we note a tendency to avoid too explicit a reference to them, in contrast to other dramatists of his time, some of whom, like Dekker, are more obviously harsh against the Papists, while others, like Jonson (a professed "recusant") and Middleton reserve their harshness for the Puritans.

All this, however, is merely on the surface of the plays, whereas in those plays we also notice a repeated insistence on the need of looking beyond outward appearances to the inner reality. Then what we find in them is that, while the dramatist seems to be directing his and our attention to other ages and nations than Elizabethan England, he is really commenting on his own age and nation. So Hamlet says of the players to Polonius, "They are the abstracts and brief chronicles of the time" (ii.2). He also goes on to illustrate the practical point of this remark in his private comment on his play-within-the-play, "The play's the thing, / wherein I'll catch the conscience of the King."

This contemporary relevance of the plays is particularly evident in those of English history, in that the dramatist, while ostensibly dramatizing events of England's mediaeval past as recorded in the Chronicles of Hall and Holinshed, invariably interprets them in the light of present events. Thus in *King John* we find Shakespeare interpreting the events of that reign in the light not only of his source-play, *The Troublesome Reign of King John*, but also of the recent fate of Mary Queen of Scots, especially in his characterization of Prince Arthur. Then in the two Parts of *Henry IV* we find an interesting parallel implied between the two rebellions, of Henry Hotspur in Part I and the Archbishop of York in Part II, and the rising of the Northern earls in 1569-70. Above all, we find an implied criticism of Elizabeth's policy in *Richard II*, especially as the old play was revived on the eve of the Essex rebellion in 1601. Then the Queen herself is said to have complained to one of her courtiers, "I am Richard II, know ye not that?"

At a deeper, less obvious level, we may notice not a few remarkable analogies with the religious situation of the time even in the comedies. The opening situation in *The Comedy of Errors*, for example, is replete with tragic possibility, in that the Syracusan merchant Aegeon is condemned to death for having all unwittingly set foot on the enemy territory of Ephesus. The contemporary analogy is here with the Catholic priests coming from Rome, who by setting foot on English soil are automatically subject to the death penalty, and for this reason they often disguised themselves as merchants – evoking the merchant in Christ's parable who comes upon "the pearl of great price" (Matt. xiii.46). Further, the very place indicated for "the death and sorry execution" of Aegeon, "behind the ditches of the abbey here" (v.1), points to Shoreditch behind the walls of the old Holywell

Priory, not far from the theatre where the play was acted, and where a Catholic priest, William Hartley, was executed at the time of the Armada in 1588.

This association, moreover, between a merchant and a priest recurs in the hero of *The Merchant of Venice*, Antonio, who is likewise shown on the point of undergoing legal execution at the insistence of Shylock the Jew. From the outset there appears something mysterious about him, from his opening words, "In sooth, I know not why I am so sad." A possible reason for this sadness, in view of the "subtext" of the play, is that it was a major task of Catholic priests working in England to provide for the future of their mission by sending promising young men abroad for their Catholic education to Rheims or Rome. Further, the place to which Bassanio wishes to go with Antonio's assistance is named Belmont, recalling the home of Southampton's cousin, Thomas Pounde of Belmont, who had persuaded Campion to write his "Letter to the Lords of the Council", and who spent most of his life in prison for his faith. It is significant that in the preliminary conversation between Bassanio and Portia at Belmont there is a riddling exchange replete with reference to the sufferings of English Catholics. When Portia exclaims at "these naughty times (which) put bars between the owners and their rights," Bassanio pleads, "Let me choose, / for as I am I live upon the rack," but Portia takes him up, "Upon the rack, Bassanio? Then confess / what treason there is mingled with your love" (iii.2). Above all, in the contrast between Antonio and Shylock, the former is explicitly described by his friend as "one in whom / the ancient Roman honour more appears / than any that draws breath in Italy", whereas in the characterization of Shylock not a few scholars have seen points of resemblance with the Puritans – such as their sobriety and severity, their frequent allusions to the Bible, their withdrawal from the fellowship of others, their practice of usury, and above all their cruelty to the Catholics, partly in revenge for their past ill-treatment at the hands of the Catholics in Mary's time. In such a context the Elizabethan audience might have recognized a deep but daring relevance in Portia's famous appeal for mercy.

Another comedy which is full of such relevance is *As You Like It*, with its setting in the Forest of Arden – not just the Ardennes in France, as in the source romance of Lodge's *Rosalynde*, but the similarly named forest in Shakespeare's Warwickshire. From the outset we hear of exiles from the court, where "the old duke is banished, and three or four loving lords have put themselves into voluntary exile with him", and whither "many young gentlemen flock to him every day". Such was the situation in Elizabethan England after the accession of Queen Elizabeth, when the Catholics found themselves increasingly oppressed by the penal laws and felt obliged by conscience to take refuge abroad, particularly to the Low Countries, not far from the original setting of the play in the Ardennes. The resulting conflict even within the same family between the victorious Protestants and the defeated Catholics may be seen in the conflicts among the brothers in this play between Duke Senior and the usurping Duke Frederick, and between Oliver and Orlando. Here, too, more than in any other of Shakespeare's plays, there is frequent nostalgic reference to "the golden world" of the past (i.1), when in "better days" the exiles "have with holy bell been knolled to church" (ii.7), days which are represented above all in the character of the good old servant Adam, in whom Orlando admires "the constant service of the antique world, when service sweat for duty, not for meed" (ii.3). In the surroundings of the forest, moreover, mention is made of "an old religious uncle" of Rosalind, "a nook merely monastic" (iii.2), and of another "old religious man" who succeeds in converting the usurping duke on his coming to the forest with an army in pursuit of his brother. (v.4)

Turning to the four great tragedies, from the beginning of *Hamlet* one is impressed with the contrast between the old order as remembered by Hamlet from the days of his father and the new order as represented by Claudius assisted by Polonius. Though Hamlet has been educated at Wittenberg, Luther's university (which wasn't founded till 1502), he feels out of place in the new order, especially once he has confronted the ghost of his father. The latter claims to have come from the Catholic purgatory, where he is "confined to fast in fires, / till the foul crimes done in my days of nature / are burnt and purged away" (i.5). The play interestingly develops into a kind of spying match, in which Claudius, prompted by Polonius, spies on Hamlet, while the latter uses the play-within-the-play to spy on his uncle so as to "catch the conscience of the King" (ii.2). In the same way, an elaborate spy system was devised in Elizabethan England by the Queen's secretary, Sir William Cecil, Lord Burghley (who seems to be parodied in Polonius), chiefly for use against Catholics at home and abroad, while the Catholics on their side, especially the Jesuits under Robert Persons, set up a counter-intelligence network through friends in the Low Countries. In particular, one may note the anguish of Hamlet at having to keep his thoughts to himself, "But break, my heart, for I must hold my tongue!" (i.2), and his concern at the end of the play that the truth be reported faithfully to "the yet unknowing world", considering what Bassanio calls "the seeming truth which cunning times put on / to entrap the wisest" (iii.2).

The same situation is repeated in Macbeth's Scotland, a situation which is reflected not in the historical sources of the play but in contemporary England. Here we find an atmosphere of fear, mistrust and secrecy, in which men have to speak to each other in riddling words for fear of spies and informers. Thus Lennox speaks darkly to a certain lord, saying, "My former speeches have but hit your thoughts, / which can interpret further" (iii.6). The same feeling of mistrust enters into the strange scene in which Macduff comes to Malcolm in England only to find himself subjected to various tests before he can finally be trusted. (iv.3)

Of all the tragedies, however, the clearest contemporary relevance of this kind appears in *King Lear*, for all its outward trappings of pre-Christian or pre-historic Britain. Here, too, as in *As You Like It*, the good are all driven into exile, not only saintly characters like Cordelia and Edgar, but also their sinning but increasingly repentant fathers Lear and Gloucester. Edgar, above all, appears in the character of a hunted priest, against whom proclamations are given out, his picture is copied and widely distributed, the ports are carefully watched, intelligence is given concerning his whereabouts, till he is driven to disguise himself even as a mad beggar. In his pretended madness, moreover, he uses words which the dramatist has borrowed from the anti-Catholic book by Samuel Harsnet, *A Declaration of Egregious Popish Impostures* (1603), which deals with the exorcizing activities of a group of Catholic priests, including a fellow Stratfordian Robert Debdale (executed in 1586). In particular, Edgar's concern to save his father reflects the spiritual purpose of the hunted priests to work for the salvation of their countrymen at the risk even of their own lives. Above all, the excessively tragic conclusion of the play may well have been prompted by the desperate situation of the English Catholics about the time of the Gunpowder Plot of 1605. Thus when Cordelia returns from France to Britain at the head of an army, reminiscent of the Spanish Armada of 1588, she protests, as did the Catholics at that time, "No blown ambition doth our arms incite, / but love, dear love, and our aged father's right" (iv.4). Subsequently, when she finds her army defeated, she utters the sad comment, with apparent reference to Shakespeare's time, "We are not the first, / who with best meaning have incurred the worst" (v.3). The final words of Kent on the dying Lear point all too clearly to the typical torture used by the English authorities on the arrested priests, "He hates him, / that would upon the rack of this tough world / stretch him out longer" (v.3).

There follows an impressive contrast between these grim tragedies and the subsequent tragi-comedies, which all end on a note of blissful reconciliation. In these plays we find the dramatist looking away as it were from the harsh reality of his contemporary world to a religious ideal, which he envisages in terms of a reunion between father and daughter, as though prolonging the moving scene of reunion between Lear and Cordelia (iv.7). The first such play is the fragmentary *Pericles*, with the miraculous reunion between the aged hero and, first, his long-lost daughter Marina, then with his wife Thaisa, whom he has seen buried at sea amid a storm. The next is *Cymbeline*, with the reunion between another British King Cymbeline and his unjustly exiled daughter Imogen, with a further emphasis on reunion between Britain and Rome, in the King's concluding command, "Let / a British and a Roman ensign wave / friendly together!" (v.5). The third is *The Winter's Tale*, with the reunion between the repentant King Leontes and, first, his long-lost daughter Perdita, then his wrongly accused wife Hermione, who appears to him as it were miraculously risen from the dead. In this we may note a marked parallel between Hermione with her appeal to the oracle of Apollo at Delphos and Catherine of Aragon with her appeal to Rome, which is actually dramatized in Shakespeare's last history play of *Henry VIII*.

This common quality in Shakespeare's last plays seems to suggest something deep in his own life. It is about this time that we notice a concern on his part to spend more of his time in his country home of Stratford, where his favourite daughter Susanna's name was recorded in the recusant lists for 1606, in the search for Catholic recusants in the wake of the Gunpowder Plot – just as his father John's name had been recorded in the same lists for 1592. Shortly afterwards, we find two of the later plays, *King Lear* and *Pericles*, both recently published in quarto, presented by a group of Catholic players at some recusant houses in Yorkshire in the years 1609-10. In this connection we may add the evidence supplied by a seventeenth-century Anglican clergyman of the district, Richard Davies, concerning the dramatist's end, that "he died a Papist" – perhaps reconciled to the old faith after a long, anguished consideration that transpires in his great tragedies. At least, we may say that the impression conveyed by his last plays is one of deep religious peace, coming as a result of reconciliation.

In this outcome we may well perceive the inner secret of Shakespeare's dramatic genius. It isn't just that he happened to be more gifted than any of his fellow countrymen with literary genius, but that, with his genius, he was a sincere seeker after a spiritual and religious ideal which he found, in spite of all the personal and political problems besetting him, in a return to the religious and Christian tradition of England and Europe – in a word, of Christendom. It was of this tradition that he had for a time been deprived, though one may well conjecture that he had never rejected it. To it also he may well have been referring in the words which he puts into the mouth of Friar Francis in *Much Ado About Nothing*, "What we have we prize not to the worth / while we enjoy it, but being lacked and lost, / why, then we rack the value, then we find / the virtue that possession would not show us / while it was ours" (iv.1).

PART II – FIVE ASPECTS

Chapter 1

THE WIVES OF HENRY VIII

The name of Henry VIII, with all his bloated bulk, towers above the pages of English history, now as the popular "bluff King Hal" of Protestant legend, now as the terrible tyrant or "Blue-Beard" of England with his six ill-fated wives. True, from the time of his accession to the English throne in 1509 he did enjoy a measure of popularity, coming as he did on the heels of the unpopular, miserly, penny-pinching Henry VII. True, from that time onwards he became in the eyes of the fond Erasmus a munificent patron of humanists and a prince of peace, thanks in no small measure to the kindly influence of his first Queen, Catherine of Aragon. And true, during that time – in contrast to his contemporary ruler of France, the notorious womanizer Francis I – he remained moderately true to his good Queen. But then "another woman" came on the scene in the person of the young lady-in-waiting to Catherine of Aragon, Anne Boleyn – the kind of woman concerning whom the French cynically remark in such a problematic situation, "*Cherchez la femme!*"

It was from then onwards that Henry began to look round for a divorce, pleading a troubled conscience concerning Catherine, since she had previously been wife to his elder brother Arthur before the latter's untimely death. On this score, however, Shakespeare makes the cynical comment put into the mouth of the Duke of Suffolk in his final history play of *Henry VIII*, "His conscience has crept too near another lady" (ii.2). For himself Henry might have been satisfied to keep Anne as his mistress, as he had already honoured Anne's elder sister Mary and perhaps

60

even their mother Elizabeth (of whom he is said to have begotten Anne*), but Anne would be content with nothing short of wife and Queen in place of Catherine. Thus it was that "the King's great matter" was spawned, namely the long and complicated proceedings for the royal divorce. This Clement VII, the Pope of the time, was unwilling to grant, partly for canonical reasons, to uphold the validity of the dispensation granted by his predecessor Alexander VI, partly because of the over-swaying power of Catherine's nephew, the Emperor Charles V. So the King allowed himself to be persuaded by his new minister, the Machiavellian Thomas Cromwell, to take the matter into his own hands, not only the divorce but also the concomitant claim to possess supreme power over the Church within his own realm.

Here precisely we may locate the turning-point between the foregoing popularity of bluff King Hal, with his no less popular Queen Kate, and the gathering tyranny which he developed not only out of his desire for a divorce from Catherine and a new marriage with Anne but also out of a compulsive obsession to have all his leading subjects, both clergy and laity, to approve these measures under a solemn oath. Many were ready to temporize with their consciences and to swear an oath which in their

---

* The reference is to a rumour that was current among the Catholic exiles on the continent concerning the birth of Anne, whose date is still uncertain. The rumour was recorded by the Catholic theologian Dr Nicholas Sander in his *De Origine ac Progressu Schismatis Anglicani* (posthumously published in 1585), that Anne was not only the second wife to Henry VIII but also his daughter by Elizabeth Boleyn. This rumour is generally discounted by historians, who hardly ever mention it, but it was justified by the first English translator of Sander's book, David Lewis, in his lengthy Introduction as published by Burns & Oates in 1877. More recently, the matter has been investigated from a medical as well as historical point of view by Peter Richard Butcher in his monograph *Where Credit is Due*, published by the Reigate Press in 1994, in which he gives the credit of fatherhood not to Henry but to Thomas Howard, Duke of Norfolk, brother to Elizabeth and uncle to Anne Boleyn. As for Shakespeare, he might well have been aware of the rumour in taking up the continuation of *Pericles*, but he would hardly have known of the fact.

heart of hearts they knew to be wrong, and so they committed themselves to the party of the King in spiritual as well as political and personal affairs. They were all the more ready to do so once they had evidence of the penalties attached to a refusal of the oath, especially after the passing of the Act of Treason by Parliament in 1535. As for the precise nature of those penalties, they were shown for all the world to see in the public executions of the two principal men of the realm who had stood out against the taking of the oath, if only by their silence, namely the wise Sir Thomas More and the holy Bishop John Fisher. It didn't matter that More had up till recently been the King's "darling" and Lord Chancellor in succession to the disgraced Cardinal Wolsey, or that Fisher had been Chancellor of Cambridge University before being appointed Bishop of Rochester. Both were on the side of Queen Catherine and of the Pope in Rome, both had refused to take the oath and were consequently enemies of the King and his new Queen, and both were to suffer for their allegiance by dying a traitor's death in the form of beheading on Tower Hill in 1535. Nor were they the only victims of the King's anger, for they had already been preceded by the monks of the London Charterhouse, who were all made examples of what would befall any who might disobey the King's decree.

This is all so serious, so tragic. It is also the way Shakespeare (if it is Shakespeare) introduces his final history play or romance of *Henry VIII* in the words of the Prologue,

> I come no more to make you laugh. Things now
> That bear a weighty and a serious brow,
> Sad, high and working, full of state and woe,
> Such noble scenes as draw the eyes to flow,
> We now present.

The play is indeed a serious and a tragic one, especially in so far as it concerns poor Catherine, about whose part Dr Johnson gave the judgment that "The genius of Shakespeare comes in and goes out with Catherine." What Johnson failed to notice, however, but what subsequent scholars from the time of James Spedding in the mid-Victorian era have noticed, is that not only the genius but also the authorship of Shakespeare goes out with Catherine, and that the ending of the play is a patchwork attributable in part to the younger dramatist of the King's Men, John Fletcher. It is the latter who contrived to turn the professed tragedy into a tragi-comedy, with the sad ending of Catherine transformed into a happy ending for Henry and Anne with their new-born infant daughter Elizabeth, while overlooking the historical fact that within a year of that birth Anne would herself become a victim of Henry's anger in 1536.

Here we have two tragedies involving the first two wives of Henry VIII, with Catherine divorced and Anne beheaded, the one so soon after the other. Already in the very year of Anne's execution Catherine, too, had died – seemingly of natural causes, but perhaps, it was rumoured, of poison administered to her at the behest of Anne. On the other hand, in the case of Henry himself one may find something at once comic and tragic. First, how was he tragic? After all, he had been obliged to endure the shame of a prolonged official trial before the eyes of the world, centering on the marital relations between himself and his first wife, then between her and her first husband, his elder brother Arthur. The main question was, Had the original marriage, broken off so abruptly by his brother's death, been consummated or not? If it had been duly consummated, there might well be doubt concerning the validity even of a papal dispensation. Then the trial was so long protracted on the advice of Pope Clement VII in the hope that Henry would lose patience and tire of his negotiations for an annulment which the Pope was in no position to grant. In consequence Henry had been nudged, urged and all but obliged to go against his traditional instincts as "Defender of the Faith" and break with the papacy and the Church of Rome, at the combined insistence of those two Thomases, Cromwell and Cranmer, with the support of Anne Boleyn. Then he was further encouraged to put all who opposed him, even such loyal servants as More and Fisher, to death by beheading – a concession not granted to others like the monks of Charterhouse, who had to endure the full horrors of a traitor's death by being hanged, drawn and quartered in full view of a crowd for the sake of "example". Then Henry went on at the further enticing of Cromwell to destroy all the holy shrines and monasteries of the realm in the name of "reformation", but in fact for the augmentation of the royal treasury. He had been assured by Cromwell that he would thus become the richest man in Christendom. And so he did for a time, till with characteristic prodigality he managed to go through it all, what with the waging of costly wars against France, the building of royal palaces and the forging of golden suits of armour for his vain indulgence in outmoded tournaments. And so the treasury was left empty for his boy successor by the time he died in 1547. This was all tragic not just for Catherine, for More and Fisher and the Carthusian monks, for the Church of Rome and the Church of England, but also for Anne, who was beheaded in 1536, for Cromwell, who was beheaded in 1540, and for Cranmer, who was burnt at the stake as a heretic under Queen Mary in 1556. But the first and most tragic victim of them all was Henry.

Then if he was so tragic, how was he comic? Well, no small part of Henry's tragedy was, as I have hinted, the way he made himself such an egregious ass, a laughing-stock in the eyes of the world in a way no husband wants to be made, least of all in a century when this was the stock-in-trade of jokes. From the writings even of so great a saint and martyr as Sir Thomas More to those of so great a dramatist as William Shakespeare, the typical joke of the sixteenth century was that made at the expense of a cuckold, a husband unable to restrain the illicit sexual drives of his wife or to refrain from the suspicion of jealousy – as we see in the tragic case of Othello, who may well have been modelled on Henry, or in the comic case of Master Ford in *The Merry Wives of Windsor*. So we have the funny rhyme, or mnemonic for remembering the order of Henry's six wives and their respective fates, "Divorced, beheaded, died. / Divorced, beheaded, survived." Of these, the two fated to be divorced were Catherine of Aragon and Anne of Cleves, the two fated to be beheaded (and so divorced on the ground of adultery) were Anne Boleyn and Catherine Howard, while the one fated to die was Jane Seymour, who died of puerperal fever soon after giving birth to Henry's only legitimate son and heir Edward, leaving Catherine Parr to survive her terrible husband, not without having to endure the fear of being burnt at the stake as a heretic.

This was all, no doubt, tragic for each of Henry's wives, and it was no less tragic for Henry himself. But what was tragic for him was comic for innumerable others, as long as they could afford to look on the contemporary scene with an objective, critical eye. After all, the two wives whom he had beheaded both suffered on the charge of adultery, which may have been largely a matter of suspicion in the case of Anne Boleyn but was all too manifest in the case of Catherine Howard. In their punishment after a public trial it was as if Henry was proclaiming before the world, like one of Shakespeare's fools, "Look at me, a cuckold!" and "Laugh at me, if you dare!" Indeed people could only laugh at him behind their sleeves, though laugh at him they surely did. As for the two divorces, the first from Catherine of Aragon called for the publication of the most intimate details of her two marriages, while evoking in the public mind a widespread suspicion of Henry's illicit relations with Anne Boleyn as his whore, while the second from Anne of Cleves was forced through on the mere basis of Henry's dislike of her whom he called "the Flanders mare", after the royal marriage had been expedited by Cromwell in the absence of the bride for the purpose of ensuring a Protestant succession. This all conspired to make Henry appear in the eyes of Europeans as at once the British Blue-Beard and the quintessential cuckold of Tudor jest-books.

Yet all the time Henry was maintaining that his one aim through marriage after marriage was the begetting of a male heir. That was eventually what he received from Jane Seymour, whom he genuinely loved but who was snatched away from him so soon after giving birth to the longed-for male heir, the sickly Edward. Till then he had received but one daughter, Mary, from Catherine of Aragon, and another, Elizabeth, from Anne Boleyn. But that was all. From the first three wives he had only two daughters and one son, but from the other three wives none. This gives us the other funny rhyme about Henry's marriages in the form of a clerihew, "The fates / fought against Henry the Eighth. / For every marriage / he got only half a child on average." Of these three children, moreover, Edward succeeded his father in 1547 but only ruled over England for six years. Mary succeeded him in 1553 but only ruled over England for another five years. Only Elizabeth, who succeeded Mary in 1558, ruled over England for forty-five years but, as the vaunted Virgin Queen, she had no children to succeed her on the throne. And so the Tudor dynasty from Wales came to a fruitless end, only to be followed by the Stuart dynasty from Scotland, which also came to a fruitless end in 1714, when Queen Anne died after some seventeen children had preceded her to the grave.

Anyhow, to return to "the six wives of Henry VIII", it may be of interest to record that two books on this subject, with the same title as that just given, were published in England within a year of each other by two authors, Alison Weir in 1991 and Antonia Fraser in 1992, each apparently in ignorance of what the other was doing. Not that they were the first to deal with the subject under that title, but already as early as 1937 one Paul Rival had come out with his own (presumably male) version of *The Six Wives of Henry VIII*. For my present purpose, however, it is enough for me to have made mention of these three books, with special recommendation of the two by the female authors. But now, leaving them all on one side, I come to state my preference for yet another work with a more general title, which is much older than any of them and will inevitably be dismissed as old-fashioned and out-of-date. Nowadays, alas, as Shakespeare's duke-turned-friar sadly comments in *Measure for Measure*, "Novelty is only in request" – even or especially in the academic world. The book to which I refer is John Lingard's *History of England*, which came out in ten volumes between 1819 and 1830, especially Volumes IV-VI which cover the Tudor period from the accession of Henry VII in 1485 till the death of Elizabeth I in 1603.

Why do I recommend such an antiquated book? That is a natural question calling for a natural answer. Up till the time of Lingard the standard history of England, as told (for example) by

Gilbert Burnet, in three volumes issued from 1679-1714, and by David Hume in four volumes issued from 1754-61, had followed the Protestant-Whig version of events during the sixteenth and seventeenth centuries. It was, in other words, the version promulgated by the victorious Protestants against the victimized Catholics during the period when the religious issue was dominant, and the two opposing sides, the traditional and the revolutionary, were engaged in a struggle with each other for nothing less than the soul of England. It had been largely owing to the long life of Elizabeth I under the adept direction of Sir William Cecil, Lord Burghley, and the necessary (from their viewpoint) execution of Mary Stuart in 1587, that had determined the outcome in favour of the Protestants. Then the official interpretation of these events was offered by one of the main supporters of "Dutch William", Gilbert Burnet, Bishop of Salisbury, in what came to be termed by the victorious Whigs "the great and glorious Revolution". Subsequently, in the following century the same Whig party patronized the intellectual movement of that age known as "the Enlightenment", whose principal exponent as well in philosophy as in historiography was David Hume.

Only in the early nineteenth century, therefore, when the Whig liberals paradoxically came to the support of Catholic emancipation against the conservative Tories, were the Catholics able to return to the mainstream as well of historiography as of the national life, and only in such an atmosphere of reform, which was paradoxically opposed by John Henry Newman in his Oxford Movement, was it possible for John Lingard to present the Catholic interpretation of the Protestant Reformation – not with any sectarian stridency but in a calm, balanced, rational manner, with such emphasis on the historical sources as to confound his Whig predecessors and to command the respect of his contemporaries. By himself, however, he was unable to turn the tide of the opposite interpretation, which had held sway not only among scholars but also among the educated public in England. They had all imbibed it as it were with their mothers' milk. Despite the formidable array of his ten volumes, the

Protestant-Whig version of the Reformation was received not only in England but throughout the world, till in England over the past two decades a new movement of so-called "revisionism", associated with the names of Eamon Duffy, Christopher Haigh and J J Scarisbrick, has come to undermine the self-confidence of the existing Protestant "orthodoxy". Now Lingard is once again in request, as the classic champion of the revisionists.

Incidentally, even in the nineteenth century, when Protestantism still reigned supreme in England, while imperceptibly merging into a secular patriotism under another "great" Queen, Victoria, the influence of Lingard may be traced in two subsequent authors, neither of them Catholic, who developed a more strident, impassioned response to the historical facts and their interpretation as brought to light by Lingard. The first, William Cobbett, was no historian but a political pamphleteer and a man of the people. Though he was a Protestant and remained such till the end of his life, he was so impressed by Lingard's interpretation that he went on to offer his own *History of the Protestant Reformation* in 1824, emphasizing its disastrous consequences on the lives of ordinary people in England, in contrast to what were then (in the Romantic age) coming to be regarded with nostalgia as "the good old days" of "merry England". This book of his, which might well have been neglected by the authorized historians for its lack of professional expertise, was, however, taken up by a more famous author who was, like Cobbett, no historian and no Catholic. He wasn't even an Englishman but a German philosopher, Karl Marx. When he came to explore the origins of Western capitalism for his composition of *Das Kapital* in the peaceful reading-room of the British Library, he lighted on Cobbett's *History*, to which he refers as his authority at a critical point in his exposition. It may therefore be maintained that the historical basis of world communism may be traced to two eminent Catholic authors, not only Sir Thomas More, whose *Utopia* became a classic of Communist literature with its roots in mediaeval monasticism, but also John Lingard, whose *History* was taken up by Marx through the medium of Cobbett. As for the twentieth century, well before the advent of modern "revisionism", the Catholic "amateur" historian, Hilaire Belloc, undertook an updating of Lingard's *History* with his own *History of England*, which came out in several volumes from 1925-31. Only, because of his lack of professionalism, his disdain for footnotes and his too obvious advocacy of the Catholic cause, he was neglected and even despised by the "orthodox" historians.

Anyhow, from the Catholic viewpoint, as it is at last coming to be treated with a new respect in the academic world, we may return to the wives of Henry VIII – not now to all six of them, who are too many to be considered as they each deserve, but to the first two, Catherine and Anne. In fact, of all Henry's wives they are the most interesting in themselves and the most significant for the history of their time. On the one hand, Catherine of Aragon stands out as the most faithful and the most Catholic of the wives, daughter as she was to the most Catholic King and Queen of Aragon and Castile, Ferdinand and Isabella, from whose union Spain came into being as a united kingdom. Especially when it came to "the King's great matter" of the divorce, she stood up not just for her own rights as Henry's Queen and lawfully wedded wife, but also for the rights of her daughter Mary, as lawful daughter to Henry and Catherine and next in line of succession (before the birth of Edward). Also implicit in her right and that of her daughter was the right of the Catholic Church, which had recognized the rights of both mother and daughter. Up till the end, therefore, in spite of the continual petty persecutions she had to endure from both Henry and Anne, she persisted in maintaining, like her principal supporters, More and Fisher, the claims of Catholic conscience as opposed to Henry's insistence on his own individual conscience.

On the other hand, Anne Boleyn – whether she was faithful to Henry or not remains doubtful, though her infidelity to him during their brief marriage has never been proved – stands out from the beginning of the divorce proceedings on the side of the new order, which wasn't yet precisely Protestant, though not Catholic either. All the same, in her own time she was generally recognized as supportive of the new ideas of Lutheranism, though in view of Henry's violent opposition to Luther it was prudent for her to dissemble her support. At least, she played the same game as Thomas Cromwell, the King's new vice-general in ecclesiastical affairs, and Thomas Cranmer, the King's new Archbishop of Canterbury, who was only able to come out of his Lutheran closet with the accession of Edward VI in 1547. She may have died a Catholic, as she had to. Still, it was under her remote auspices and subsequently under those of Henry's last and more recognizably Protestant wife Catherine Parr, that the Princess Elizabeth was brought up as a Protestant under Protestant tutors, so as to become the true foundress and patroness of the Church of England with the assistance of Cromwell's successor, Sir William Cecil, whose effective rule of Elizabethan England was described by Catholic authors of the time as *"regnum Cecilianum"*.

This contrast, however much it may have been covered up by the Protestant-Whig historians, with their heaping of praise on Anne and "good Queen Bess" and obloquy on Catherine and especially "bloody Mary", is what emerges in the pages of Lingard in an opposite sense. For him Anne and Elizabeth are by no means the paragons of virtue they have come to appear in the eyes of Protestant patriotism, but Catherine comes as close as any of the great women who fill the annals of Tudor history to being just such a paragon, not least during the years of her persecution under Henry. Such is, moreover, the view of her maintained in Shakespeare's *Henry VIII*, where this epithet "paragon" is used of her by Henry himself, as he professes to esteem her "before the primest creature / That's paragon'd o' the world" (ii.4). As for Mary, her cruel treatment of the Protestants opposed to her is hard even for her strongest adherents to justify, but it may be noted that this policy of hers, though supported by her bishops, was criticized by her Spanish husband, Philip II, and by her Archbishop of Canterbury, Reginald Pole. Only it has to be remembered by those who so strongly favour "Good Queen Bess" over "Bloody Mary" that Mary at least punished the Protestants under the existing laws against heresy, the same laws according to which the patriot King Henry V had punished Lollards like Sir John Oldcastle (Shakespeare's model for Sir John Falstaff), when she might have punished many of them for the crime of treason in consequence of their support of Wyatt's Rebellion. Elizabeth, however, punished Catholic priests and recusants under new-fangled laws, not as "heretics" but as "traitors", after having driven them into a position where they could hardly seem otherwise, during a period not just of four or five years but of the forty-five years of her reign.

Now I come at last to my main point, which is neither the Protestant-Whig interpretation nor yet the opposite viewpoint of John Lingard and the more recent "revisionists", but the way these four women, Catherine and Mary, Anne and Elizabeth, are introduced to us, whether directly or indirectly, in the later plays or romances of William Shakespeare. During the lifetime of Elizabeth it would have been too dangerous for him to touch at all openly on the reign of her father Henry VIII, but in speaking of the reigning Queen he occasionally stoops to such flattering descriptions of her as "the imperial votaress" in *A Midsummer Night's Dream* (ii.1), and "our gracious empress" in *Henry V* (Chorus V), and there is the flattering characterization of her as the Countess Olivia in *Twelfth Night*. But once he moves into the safer years of James I, as dramatist for the newly styled King's Men, he feels the leisure to look back to the troubled years of Henry's reign, and especially to Henry's women, culminating in the openly historical play of *Henry VIII* – though how much of the play is by Shakespeare and how much by his young collaborator John Fletcher, is open to dispute. Of Henry's six wives only the first two, Catherine and Anne, appear in the *dramatis personae*, and Catherine (as noted above) is very much the heroine till she "goes out" with the genius of Shakespeare at the end of Act IV – though in the apportioning of scenes from the time of Spedding onwards the later scenes in which she so affectingly appears are attributed not to Shakespeare but to Fletcher. Then in the final scene in which she appears, Catherine calls down God's blessing on her daughter Mary, who is however present neither in this play nor in historical fact, since she was never allowed by Henry to visit her mother even on the latter's death-bed. Then she prays, "The dews of heaven fall thick in blessings on her!" – as though recalling the meager blessing which is all Isaac has left to bestow on his son Esau, after having given everything to Jacob, "Behold thy dwelling shall be the fullness of the earth and of the dew of heaven from above" (Gen. xxvii.39). She adds that Mary "is young and of a noble modest nature" (iv.2), which is amply borne out by Lingard in his account of her reign, apart from her severe repression of heresy. As for Anne Boleyn, her characterization in the play is by no means so favourable. In the first scene in which she appears, she isn't averse to receiving the kisses of Lord Sands, then of the disguised King, to whom she is yet a stranger, and thus she is implicitly compared to the heroine of *Troilus and Cressida*, whose wanton behaviour in the Greek camp disgusts even the wily Ulysses (iv.5). In a subsequent scene between Anne and an unnamed old lady, we are shown a contrast between her affected modesty, which the old lady ironically calls her "soft cheveril conscience", and her apparent ambition, which she coyly hides beneath a mask of what the old lady again criticizes as "this spice of your hypocrisy" (ii.3). When, however, we turn to the scenes of her triumphal coronation in Act IV and the solemn christening of the Princess Elizabeth in Act V, we have evidently left Shakespeare and his genius behind, and his place has been taken by the Protestant John Fletcher (son of a former Bishop of London), who relies for his source material on John Foxe's *Book of Martyrs*, a source on which Shakespeare has never drawn in his previous plays.

On the whole, then, considering that *Henry VIII* is the last, if largely collaborative, play of Shakespeare – setting aside the similarly disputed romance of *Two Noble Kinsmen* – it is strangely unsatisfactory in matters of plot and characterization, which are commonly regarded as the *forte* of Shakespeare's dramatic genius. If the play is all by him, and there are still scholars who maintain its integrity, it is strange that what begins with the opening words of the Prologue, forecasting tragedy, should culminate in a final act with such a happy ending for Henry, his wife Anne and the baby princess Elizabeth, under the benign blessing of Cranmer, who has only just been – anachronistically – saved from his enemies by the King's intervention. It is as if we are suddenly witnessing a reversion from the Catholic interpretation, as espoused by Lingard, to the Protestant interpretation, as espoused by Gilbert Burnet, thanks in no small measure to a change of source to Foxe's *Book of Martyrs*. As for characterization, it is here scarcely in evidence, least of all in the King, who makes many long speeches assertive of his royal dignity while remaining faceless. Yet he is personally responsible for the unjust turns of fortune against his successive victims, the noble Duke of Buckingham, the eminent Cardinal Wolsey, and the majestic Catherine herself. What is more, there is no mention of the religious changes which in fact took place well before the date of the play's ending, or even of the impending fate of Anne Boleyn in the year of Catherine's death, depicted at the end of Act IV. The only mention of the success of the Protestant cause under the future Queen Elizabeth comes when Cranmer utters his prophecy in the last scene concerning the baby princess, that "God shall be truly known," which is generally ascribed by those who admit the theory of collaboration to Fletcher, not to Shakespeare.

For an understanding of how Shakespeare really saw the tragic events of Henry's reign, it is necessary for us to go back from *Henry VIII* to the foregoing final romances, which taken together may be seen as building up to that last historical romance. When we go back to *The Winter's Tale*, we find the parallel between Catherine and Hermione, and then between Henry and Leontes, so impressive – so long as we consider the plays together, unlike the common practice of editors, who prefer to regard their chosen play by itself alone. Not that Catherine is put on trial, like Hermione, for the crime of adultery, but she is put on trial at the instance of her husband for a supposed defect in their original marriage. Also like Hermione, it is emphasized that she is the daughter of a great King, and proud to be so, but she realizes there is little she can say in her own defence before such a prejudiced court, and so, like Hermione appealing to the oracle of Apollo at Delphos, she makes her appeal to the Pope at Rome. (In some of the Protestant controversial writings of this period, it may be noted, the Pope's decrees are compared, not without scorn, to the oracles of Apollo located not at Delphi or Delos but at Delphos.) As for the giving of the oracle, which so impresses the two envoys Cleomenes and Dion, they seem to be describing their impressions of a solemn High Mass at St Peter's, Rome. Then, if Hermione corresponds to Catherine, to whom should Perdita correspond but the princess Mary? For example, just as Catherine calls down a blessing from heaven on the head of Mary, Hermione also prays for such a blessing on the head of Perdita at the end of the play, "You gods, look down, / and from your sacred vials pour your graces / upon my daughter's head!" (v.3). Here, however, there is no Anne Boleyn and no princess Elizabeth. Also, in contrast to the historical fact of Henry's continued grudge against Catherine till the end, when he wouldn't even allow the princess Mary to visit her mother on her death-bed, in *The Winter's Tale* we are shown both the repentance of Leontes and his reconciliation first with Perdita, then with Hermione. Lastly, we have to consider the strange setting of the romance, which Shakespeare oddly switches from the Sicilia-Bohemia of his source, Robert Greene's pastoral romance of *Pandosto*, even to the extent of providing the land-locked Bohemia with an unhistorical coastline. Evidently, the dramatist is interested neither in Sicilia nor in Bohemia as such, but for him Sicilia, known in classical times as Trinacria, the three-cornered island, is the similarly three-cornered island of England, and for him Bohemia is the Catholic continent, whose King Polixenes is described by Leontes in his confession to prince Florizel, "You have a holy father, / a graceful gentleman, against whose person, / so sacred as it is, I have done sin" (v.1). Here, if Leontes is Henry, who can Polixenes be but the Pope?

Then, turning from *The Winter's Tale* to the preceding romance of *Cymbeline*, we find the setting is Britain in the time not just of the Romans but more precisely of the birth of Christ, as explicitly noted in Shakespeare's source, Holinshed's *Chronicles*. Here the main problem is between Cymbeline, King of Britain, and his daughter by his unnamed former wife, Imogen. Prompted by his second wife, who is also unnamed, he wishes to arrange a marriage between Imogen and his present wife's worthless son Cloten, only to learn that Imogen has already been secretly married to one Posthumus Leonatus. In his anger against his daughter, he banishes his son-in-law, who takes refuge in Rome. Given such a situation, it isn't so difficult to recognize another set of topical allusions, strangely parallel to those in *The Winter's Tale*, beginning with the obvious parallel between Cymbeline and Henry, both being kings of Britain. In this connection it may be noticed that, whereas in *King Lear* (whose hero is yet another King of Britain) there is no mention of "Britain" save as the locality of the play in the *dramatis personae*, in Cymbeline the name of "Britain" recurs no less than 26 times – maybe with the implication that Henry, being a Welsh Tudor, preferred the inclusive name of "Britain" to the exclusive name of "England", which is otherwise preferred by the dramatist himself. Then, if Imogen is Cymbeline's daughter by his first wife, she would correspond to the princess Mary, while the King's second wife would be Mary's stepmother Anne Boleyn. What is more, that second wife is significantly remembered by Cymbeline in the outcome of the play as "our wicked Queen", who has, among her other iniquities, dissuaded him from paying his customary tribute to Rome, which he now resolves to renew, in spite of having just defeated the Roman army in battle. As for Rome, it is the setting for the exile of Posthumus, where he is oddly described, in terms reminiscent of those applied by Leontes to Polixenes, as sitting "amongst men like a descended god", and as having "a kind of honour sets him off / more than a mortal seeming", and as "a sir so rare, / which you know cannot err" (i.6). In brief, Posthumus, like Polixenes, seems to stand for the Pope, with special reference to his claim of infallibility in matters of faith and morals. So his marriage with Imogen may be explained allegorically in terms of Mary's devotion to the papacy, and perhaps also with reference to her project of marriage with Reginald Pole, who while cardinal in Rome had come close (within the margin of one vote) to being elected Pope in succession to Pope Paul III in 1549. This parallelism may also explain the otherwise enigmatic saying of Imogen to Posthumus at the end of the play in their happy reunion, "Think that you are upon a rock" (v.5), with reference to the Rock of Peter on which the Church is built.

Proceeding yet further into "the backward and abyss of time" (*The Tempest* i.2), one may discern additional parallels between Henry and Othello/Lear, in that Othello is "of royal siege" (i.2) and Lear is, like Cymbeline, King of Britain, though (as noted above) the name of "Britain" fails to appear in his play. Desdemona, too, may be seen as foreshadowing Catherine both in her loyalty to her husband and in the accompaniment of the Willow Song in her final scenes with the line "A green willow must be my garland", just as Catherine in her last scene, though she is not (needless to say) murdered in bed by her husband, has a vision of celestial beings who bring her "garlands" of bays. Anyhow, the whole character of Desdemona, praised as she is by Cassio for being filled with "the grace of heaven" (ii.1), is a very anticipation of the good Catherine. The same, too, may be said of Cordelia, who is literally "the heart of Lear" (from the French *Coeur de Lear*). Beyond them the parallels with Catherine and/or Mary fade away as we move backwards from the reign of James to that of Elizabeth.

Whether these parallels convince or not, what is important is the recognition that Shakespeare as a dramatist wasn't living above the clouds in a land of his poetic or dramatic imagination, as he is traditionally seen by scholars who write in the Protestant-Whig tradition, flinching as they do from the harsh reality of the Elizabethan age and preferring the false comfort of the Elizabethan myth. All his plays are in their several ways what Hamlet calls "the abstracts and brief chronicles of the time" (ii.2). After all, how could he really be interested in the stories, whether comic or tragic, on which he erected the edifice of his plays, when there was so much of greater interest and more profound significance going on around him? He hardly needed to exert his poetic or dramatic imagination, save to recognize the hidden parallels between his sources and the events of his age, whether Elizabethan or Jacobean or Henrician. He had only to look round him and see in every county what he calls in Sonnet lxxiii "bare ruined choirs, where late the sweet birds sang." At the same time, in his plays he couldn't but look beyond those ruins to the people of his own century, from Henry to Elizabeth, from Cromwell to the two Cecils, who were responsible for them. His viewpoint, like that of Lingard, was evidently that of a Catholic, not in religious controversy against the Protestants, which he rather sought to avoid in the name of what Hamlet calls "sweet religion" (iii.4), but in opposition to the persecuting Queen and her council, particularly Sir William Cecil, Lord Burghley, alias Polonius. He thus stands out as a champion not only of the Catholic religion in his time but of all Catholic Christendom as he sees it in the culture and tradition of his native England going back to the time of St Augustine of Canterbury and Pope St Gregory I. He is also a champion, like Sir Thomas More before him, of the right of conscience to refrain (for example) from taking the oath of supremacy, which no Catholic (that is, the great majority of Englishmen throughout the sixteenth century) could take without committing perjury. From this point of view, which is neither narrow nor sectarian – as "orthodox" scholars are wont to repeat in parrot fashion – he is, again like More before him, a champion of Queen Catherine, according to that Catholic interpretation of Tudor history espoused by John Lingard.

Chapter 2

THE RENAISSANCE ACADEMY

In striking contrast to the ascendancy of Aristotle in the mediaeval university, it is Plato who emerges as the favoured philosopher of the humanists in the age of the Renaissance. The rise of Plato and Platonism in this age is above all associated with the little city of Florence among the mountains of Tuscany – such a little city, hardly known to the world at large before the coming of Dante towards the end of the thirteenth century, and relapsing into comparative insignificance after the age of Galileo in the early seventeenth century! Her height of prosperity is thus all but coterminous with the rise and fall of the Italian Renaissance, when so many of the leading figures, humanists, poets and artists, of that movement were either native to or patronized by that city.

Why, then, we may ask, did this city of Florence come to gain such a position of influence at this time? Was it just a matter of fortune in virtue of her climate and location, as her name seems to imply, "a city of flowers"? Much of the credit for its rise in the world during the fifteenth century – well after the death of Dante in 1321 – must be assigned to two great rulers, Cosimo de' Medici (1389-1464) and his grandson Lorenzo the Magnificent (1449-92). No less credit may also be assigned to the continuing menace of the Turks, culminating in the downfall of the great city of Constantinople in 1453.

Already in 1393 the Byzantine emperor Manuel II sent as his envoy to Italy, to plead for Western aid against the Turks, the Greek scholar Manuel Chrysoloras. Three years later Chrysoloras returned as teacher of Greek at the university of Florence, and thither he attracted many of the leading Italian humanists desirous of acquiring the Greek language as the fount of Western culture. In the course of his teaching he not only composed the first Greek grammar for the West, entitled *Erotemata*, but he also translated the two great epics of Homer and Plato's *Republic* into Latin. Thus he came to be hailed as founder of Greek studies in Renaissance Italy, which was no mean title considering how central the revival of Greek was to the movement of the Renaissance.

Of even greater importance to Florence and the development of Renaissance art and learning was the arrival of some seven hundred Greeks with the emperor John VIII Palaeologus for an ecumenical council of the Church, which began at Ferrara in 1438 but moved to Florence the following year at the invitation of Cosimo de' Medici. The purpose of this council wasn't only the obtaining of Western aid for the Eastern Empire against the Turks, but also the achieving of reunion between the Latins and the Greeks, who had been divided from each other since the eleventh century. At the same time, it impressed on Western scholars the need of Greek both for communicating with these cultured representatives of the Eastern Empire and for reading the Greek classics in philosophy and literature, not just in Latin translation but in the original.

After the council was over, several of the leading Greek scholars remained in Italy, and two of them in particular, John Bessarion, who was soon to be appointed cardinal of the Roman Church, and Gemistus Plethon, a lay theologian, inspired Cosimo de' Medici with the idea of founding an Academy in Florence, as distinct from the university, for the fostering of Platonic studies. Bessarion himself had written in defence of Plato against the Aristotelian scholar George of Trebizond, and Plethon also wrote a treatise on the difference between Aristotle and Plato, a work that now fired the humanists of the age with a new interest in the thought of Plato.

It was, however, only after the fall of Constantinople in 1453, though not precisely as a direct outcome of that disaster, that the Academy began to flourish under the direction of a young scholar, Marsilio Ficino (1433-99). He came to this task from a study of Aristotle and Augustine in Latin, followed by a further study of

Plato in Greek. Now the major task entrusted to him by Cosimo wasn't only the direction of the Academy but also the translation of all the works of Plato into Latin, a task which took him from 1463 to 1473, till they were finally printed in 1484. In particular, he composed a Commentary on Plato's *Symposium* on the idea of love, completed in 1469 and printed in 1484, and this soon became the principal text of Italian Neo-Platonism. He also drew parallels between Greek paganism in the light of Plato's teaching and Christianity in his treatise *De Doctrina Christiana* in 1474, while further developing his theological interpretation of Plato in his *Theologia Platonica* in 1484. These writings of his remained the standard works of Platonism in Europe till the eighteenth century, and so they may be said to contain the characteristic philosophy of the Italian Renaissance, in a combined continuity and contrast with the interpretation of Aristotle proposed by St Thomas Aquinas in the thirteenth century at the University of Paris.

Much of Ficino's work was carried out at the house provided for him by his patron on the Via Larga in Florence, but the meetings of the Academy with their inspiring discussions on Plato were held at the villas of the Medici family outside Florence, such as the Villa Careggi. Typical of Ficino's thought is what he writes on the creation of all things out of chaos by the power of divine love, in the course of his *Commentary on the Symposium*. "The still formless essence," he explains, "is what we mean by chaos, the nothing out of which all things were created. Its first turning to God is the birth of love. Its reception of the divine ray is the nourishing of love. Its illumination which follows is the growing of love. Its cleaving to God is the inrush of love. And its reception of form is love's perfection." He goes on to note that "In all worlds there is love within chaos. Love precedes every world. It awakens what is sleeping, lightens what is obscure, gives life to the dead, form to the formless, and bestows perfection on imperfect things." Such thought, for all its relation of Christian concepts to the pagan philosophy of the Greeks, was by no means secular or pagan, like that of other leading humanists in contemporary Italy, notably Lorenzo Valla, but it was deeply Christian in inspiration, and the orthodoxy of Ficino, unlike that of his successor Pico della Mirandola, was never seriously called in question. Rather, in his positive attitude towards the Greek Classics including Plato, he was but following the example of many of the old Church Fathers, Clement of Alexandria, Origen and Basil in the East, Ambrose and Augustine in the West. He was ordained priest in 1473 after mature consideration.

A new period in the fortunes of the Academy came with the arrival of another young scholar, John Pico Count della Mirandola, in 1482. From his studies of canon law at Bologna and Aristotelian philosophy at Padua, he had gone on to acquire a variety of Eastern languages, Hebrew, Chaldaic and Arabic, as well as Greek. In particular, he interested himself in the mystical writings of the Jewish Cabbala and what was then regarded as the *prisca theologia*, or primeval theology, of Hermes Trismegistus in Egypt, of Orpheus and Pythagoras in Greece. With this variety of unaccustomed learning, he went on to Rome with a quixotic proposal to defend any of nine hundred theses on all knowledge – only to find a number of them denounced to Pope Innocent VIII as heretical. He therefore judged it expedient to withdraw to the comparative safety of Florence, where he was converted to a more Christian way of thinking by the fiery Dominican Savonarola and died wearing the habit of a friar in 1494, two years after the death of his patron Lorenzo.

Ironically Pico is chiefly known to posterity not so much for all these theses as for his introductory "Oration on the Dignity of Man", which is often taken as a typical expression of Renaissance humanism and optimism. In this work he declares, "It is a commonplace of the schools that man is a little world, in which we may discern a body mingled of earthly elements and an eternal breath, the vegetable life of the plants and the intelligence of the angels with a likeness to God." And again, "Man is the intermediary among all creatures. He is familiar with the gods above him, as he is lord of the beings beneath him. By the acuteness of his senses, the inquiry of his reason, and the light of his intelligence, he is the interpreter of nature, set midway between the timeless unchanging and the flux of time." Not infrequently this passage has been identified as the source of Hamlet's enthusiastic exclamation on man, "What a piece of work is a man! How noble in reason, how infinite in faculty, in form, in moving, how express and admirable in action, how like an angel in apprehension, how like a god!" (ii.2). Pico further composed his *Heptaplus*, or discourse on the seven days of creation, to show the deep harmony of Plato with Moses, and of Greek paganism with Christianity, besides the mutual harmony between Aristotle and Plato. His collected works were published after his death by his nephew John Francis under the title of *Commentationes* (1495-96), with a prefatory *Life of John Picus Earl of Mirandola*, which was translated into English in 1510 by Thomas More. In this *Life* Pico is described as "a desirous searcher of the secrets of nature", who "left the common trodden paths and gave himself wholly to speculation and philosophy as well human as divine". It is also said of him, not without blame, that he particularly sought out "the secret mysteries of the Hebrews, Chaldees and Arabians, and many things drawn out of the old obscure philosophy of Pythagoras, Trismegistus and Orpheus, and many other things strange" – which ended in his undoing at Rome.

The influence of this Academy soon spread beyond the confines of Florence, and not only as far as Rome. It was on the occasion of a banquet held at the Villa Careggi on the supposed birthday of Plato, November 7, 1474, that the idea of love, so enthusiastically praised by Ficino in his commentary on Plato's *Symposium*, inspired a young poet Girolamo Benivieni to compose his *Canzone del Amore Celeste e Divino*. To this poem Pico added a long commentary of his own, which was in turn taken up by another leading Italian humanist, Pietro Bembo, subsequently an eminent cardinal at the court of the Medici Pope Leo X, in his ideal discussions on love in the gardens of Asolo, entitled *Gli Asolani*. Then the Neo-Platonist courtier Baldassare Castiglione was inspired to compose his popular presentation of the ideal courtier *Il Cortegiano* in 1528, with Bembo himself as the main interlocutor. It was this book which chiefly introduced the ideas of Italian Neo-Platonism to

Elizabethan England, when it was translated into English by Sir Thomas Hoby in 1561. Its influence may be seen in the title of a book by the explorer Sir Humphrey Gilbert published in 1570 under the title, *Queen Elizabeth's Academy* (of chivalry, policy and philosophy), where the royal court itself is seen as a Platonic Academy. Finally, these ideas are given supreme literary form in English by the representative poet of the age, Edmund Spenser, in his "Hymn of Heavenly Love", one of the *Four Hymns* published in 1590.

> Love, lift me up upon thy golden wings
> From this base world unto thy heaven's height,
> Where I may see those admirable things
> Which there thou workest with thy sovereign might,
> Far above feeble reach of earthly sight.

Meanwhile, in the decline of the Academy at Florence, we find other academies springing up and multiplying in Renaissance Italy, though inevitably they became institutionalized and politicized. First, in 1498 Cardinal Bessarion established the *Accademia Romana di Storia e di Archeologia* in Rome. Then in 1582, under the long-term influence of Cardinal Bembo, though long after his death in 1547, there appeared the *Accademia della Crusca* in Florence for the purifying of the Italian language, based on the Tuscan dialect of Dante. Then at the beginning of the following century in 1603, there appeared back in Rome the *Accademia dei Lincei*, with Galileo as its most distinguished member. These were but a few of many such academies.

Turning now from Italy to England, and from Florence in the fifteenth century to London in the early sixteenth, it wasn't just through Hoby's translation of Castiglione that the ideas of Italian Neo-Platonism were first introduced to England, but already in the second half of the fifteenth century we find a stream of young English scholars making their way to that little city for the study of Greek. First, the two forerunners of the New Learning in England, William Grocyn and Thomas Linacre, made their way to Florence in the late 1480s, to study Greek under the humanist Angelo

Poliziano. While Linacre went on to specialize in medicine, Grocyn returned to Oxford to introduce the study of Greek at that university, and among his first students he numbered the young Thomas More, as well as Erasmus and John Colet. As for Colet, he made his own journey to France and Italy in the 1490s, where he may well have met Ficino and Pico, and he was deeply influenced by the austere Savonarola. On his return to Oxford, he gave his celebrated lectures on St Paul's Epistle to the Romans, with little reference to the scholastic thinkers, but with many citations from St Augustine, Origen, Dionysius, Plato and Plotinus, with long passages from Ficino and Pico as leading Platonists. The tale is often told of a conversation he had at that time with Erasmus, in which he effectively persuaded the latter to give up his study of Aquinas and to turn rather to the Scriptures and the Fathers. With Erasmus and More he is numbered by Seebohm among the "Oxford reformers", but it was rather in London that the three men became close friends and variously influenced each other in a movement of humanist, not Protestant, reform.

In these men we may recognize early signs of the influence of Florentine Platonism in England, but the first "academy" as such is to be seen in the household of Sir Thomas More, first at Bucklersbury in London, and then from 1523 onwards at his new home in Chelsea. Of that household in Chelsea Erasmus speaks in glowing terms in one of his letters. "You would say," he wrote, "there were in that place Plato's academy. But I do the house injury in comparing it to Plato's academy, wherein there were only disputations of geometrical figures and numbers, and sometimes of moral virtues. I should rather call his home a school or university of Christian religion. For there is none therein but reads or studies the liberal sciences, their special care is piety and virtue." As for the members of this little academy, they were, to begin with, More's own children, his son John, his three daughters, Margaret, Cecily and Elizabeth, his step-daughter Alice, his foster daughter Margaret Gigs, his maid Dorothy Colly, together with their spouses as they came to marry, and their various tutors. It was an academy notable for its number of women, concerning whom More held advanced views on the propriety of providing women with a higher education. In this education, moreover, he laid as much emphasis on Greek as on Latin, and on the way of sweetness and love rather than of punishment.

More himself never went to Italy or Florence for the study of Greek, but what he began at Oxford under Grocyn he continued for himself in London. There one of his humanist friends was William Lily, who was teaching Greek in the city before being appointed by Colet the first headmaster of his newly founded St Paul's School. Subsequently, on the occasion of the founding of a Greek Chair at Corpus Christi College, Oxford, with More's protégé John Clement as its first occupant in 1518, there arose fierce opposition from a group of self-styled "Trojans" against the teaching of Greek, and then More in his function as steward of the university went to Oxford to defend the pursuit of Greek studies and a liberal education. Like Colet, he was also a keen Platonist, though not to the extent of opposing Aquinas and Aristotle. His Platonism is to be seen in his frequent use of the dialogue form, as in his (Latin) *Utopia*, modelled in part on Plato's *Republic*, his *Dialogue of Heresies* against the English Lutheran William Tyndale, and his *Dialogue of Comfort against Tribulation*, which he wrote during his imprisonment in the Tower of London in 1534. He may also be seen as spreading the ideal of Platonic humanism through his many friendships, with which he formed a kind of human network, including almost all the leading humanists in England and Northern Europe. But alas, this was brought to an untimely end by the religious policy of Henry VIII and his reign of terror from 1534 onwards, though the sweet memory of More continued to be cherished all the more dearly by his many descendants and the Catholic recusants.

Meanwhile, it may be asked, what about the neighbouring realm of France in between Italy and England? The prestige of Paris University, with its continuing emphasis on Aristotelian philosophy, was as high as ever during this period. Yet there were also not a few humanists in France, such as Lefèvre d'Etaples, who visited Italy many times in the 1490s and studied both the

Greek classics and Neo-Platonic mysticism. But there was as yet no institution calling itself an "academy" till 1570, when the first French academy was founded by a member of the poetic circle "La Pléiade", Jean Antoine de Baif, with the help of his friends and the encouragement of the Queen regent, Catherine de' Medici. This was later taken over by Catherine's son Henri III and made the Palace Academy. At the same time a similar academy was established by the Huguenot leader Henri de Navarre, as described in a letter of 1583 to England. The idea behind these developments was explained by the Huguenot Pierre de la Primaudaye in his book entitled *The French Academy*, which was translated into English by Thomas Bowes and went into several editions from 1586 onwards. It took the form of discussions among four noblemen of Anjou, centering on the Greek ideal of self-knowledge. It is seen by many Shakespeare scholars as a probable source for *Love's Labour's Lost*, which indeed opens with the ideal of "a little academe" to be established in the kingdom of Navarre by the King and three of his nobles, whose names interestingly echo those of Catholic and Huguenot leaders in the wars of religion.

The subsequent development of this ideal during the seventeenth century, both in England and in France, no less than in Italy, follows the inevitable path of institutionalization, politicization, and secularization. In France we see the establishment of the famous *Académie Française* by Cardinal Richelieu in 1635, and in England that of the Royal Society under Charles II in 1662. In both cases the principal aim of the academy was, like the Italian *Accademia della Crusca*, the purification of the language according to the simplified ideals of a new, scientific age.

In conclusion, it is interesting to note (with Shakespeare in *All's Well That Ends Well* ii.1) how "great floods have flown from simple sources". Thus in classical Athens we see how the conversations of Socrates and his friends were set down and developed by Plato in the form of dialogue, and further institutionalized in his Academy, by the side of other Athenian schools in other locations. Similarly, in Renaissance Florence we see how the private studies of Ficino on Plato and Plotinus came to be disseminated in the intellectual discussions of the Academy at the villas of the Medici family, how they were idealized in the writings of Benivieni, Bembo and Castiglione, and how they were eventually institutionalized in the various academies of Italy, France and England, as it were by the side of, if at times in opposition to, the continuing universities. Thus the very word "academy" may be taken as standing for the educational ideal of the Renaissance, or at least for the philosophical ideal at the heart of the Renaissance. It may also be seen as contrasted no less with the disputatious schools of the mediaeval universities than with the argumentative controversies spawned by the Protestant Reformation, and as offering an oasis of academic peace and heavenly harmony, according to the aim of Platonic philosophy to rise on the wings of love, culminating in the ecstasy proposed by Plato and Plotinus as the height of mystical comtemplation in what Plotinus called "the flight of the alone to the Alone".

Chapter 3

THE GREAT CONTROVERSY

The word "controversy" isn't exactly a popular word nowadays. In the modern world we try to avoid disputes, quarrels, controversies. We want to be friends with each other, to understand each other, to enter into what is called "dialogue" with each other. In this age of "globalization" there should be no room for friction, for difference, for any form of confrontation or discrimination. Even if there is to be a debate, as between two political parties, or two factions within one party, it has to be conducted in a friendly manner, so as to tone down any feeling of animosity or rivalry.

Least of all, we think, should there be any controversy concerning religion. In this respect, today's keywords are "ecumenism" and "inter-religious dialogue". In particular, the Christian world during the past fifty years has been dominated by the Second Vatican Council, which gathered together the Catholic bishops of the whole world with other religious leaders in the 1960s. One of its earliest and most influential documents was that concerning "ecumenism" among the Christian denominations, while other documents concerned the relations between the Catholic Church and other religions. Subsequently, a special agency, or "dicastery", was established at the Vatican under the name of "Pontifical Council for Inter-Religious Dialogue".

What a great difference there is between such developments in the Catholic Church during the past fifty years and those we find prevailing in the same Church some 450 years ago at the time of the Council of Trent! That Council met during the period from 1545 to 1563, and it was chiefly concerned with facing the challenge of the Protestant Reformation. Then, instead of dialogue on the part of the reformers, from Luther onwards there was only confrontation. Then, too, instead of unity according to the stated ideal of Christ himself, there appeared a rift in Western Christendom between Catholic and Protestant that has remained till today. From then onwards there appeared in all the nations of the West not just confrontation and opposition but religious warfare and controversy. Eventually, in the mid-seventeenth century there took place the Peace of Westphalia in 1648, by which the disastrous Thirty Years' War in the Holy Roman Empire was brought to an end, and then those nations turned to a more secular ideal.

This secular ideal of peace is commonly seen as anticipated in the plays of William Shakespeare, who paradoxically flourished in an age when the religious disputes in England were at their height. His own parents and grandparents had been witnesses to the far-reaching religious changes that had taken place under the successive Tudor monarchs, from Henry VIII to Elizabeth I. First, Henry had broken away from Rome and established an independent Church of England, while still opposing the new Lutheran ideas and maintaining the traditional Catholic teaching. Next, his son Edward favoured the Protestant reformers during the six years of his rule, but Henry's elder daughter Mary restored the country to union with Rome and the profession of the Catholic faith. She, however, only reigned for five years, and when she died, she was succeeded by her half-sister Elizabeth, who re-established the Church of England in line with her brother's reforms and the "reformed Churches" on the continent. From then onwards what is called "the Elizabethan settlement" (in a Protestant sense) prevailed for the forty-five years of Elizabeth's reign, till what had been a largely Catholic country under Mary may be said to have become a Protestant nation.

All these changes in religion had taken place in England by the time Shakespeare was born in Stratford-upon-Avon in 1564. And by the time he entered upon his career as a dramatist in London about the year 1590 it may be said that England was at least officially committed to Protestantism. All this time, needless to say, various controversies turning on the religious issue had been taking place, and they may even be said to have reached a climax during the period of Shakespeare's dramatic career, which may be roughly dated from 1590 to 1610. What is more, it was no small part of the Queen's policy, with the adroit assistance of her chief adviser Sir William Cecil, Lord Burghley, to repress those controversies, whether on the Catholic or the Puritan side, by a strict censorship. After all, in those days religion wasn't regarded, as it is today, as a matter of private opinion, but it had all kinds of political implications and reverberations.

Such is the setting within which Shakespeare came to write the plays concerning which his friend Ben Jonson declared that they were "not of an age but for all time". It was indeed a setting of fierce religious controversy, not only between Catholic and Protestant, but also among Protestants between the more moderate Anglicans, who supported the religious changes, and the more radical Puritans, who considered that the changes hadn't gone far enough. Yet in his plays Shakespeare seems to keep clear of all controversial issues, as it were "sitting on the fence", or rather attending to what seemed to him common to all members of his audience, whatever might be their religious persuasion. If anything, he seems to be anti-Puritan, if only because the Puritans were the avowed enemies of the theatre. On the whole, however, he may be said to have kept his religious and political ideas to himself, as being the wisest attitude for him to take in the circumstances.

There are indeed a few indications in his plays pointing to his attitude not so much to religion as to religious controversy. First, one may recall the exasperated reaction in *Romeo and Juliet* of Romeo's friend Mercutio on being mortally wounded by Juliet's cousin Tybalt in a duel which he has taken up on Romeo's behalf. "A plague," he exclaims, "on both your houses!" (iii.1). In these words, of course, he isn't speaking of any religious controversy but only of the strife between the houses of Montague and Capulet which is the setting for this tragedy. But in the setting of Elizabethan England such strife all too often took on a religious character, and the name of Montague, while being that of Romeo's family in the Italian story, also happened to be that of a prominent Catholic recusant family in Sussex. Accordingly, not a few scholars have seen in the words of Mercutio an indirect expression of the dramatist's own feelings about the religious strife of his own time in England.

All the same, we may wonder, how can we be sure if that is what the dramatist really meant in those words of Mercutio? Of course, we can't be sure, if we take the words by themselves, but in the contemporary comedy of *A Midsummer Night's Dream* we come upon a similar statement which the dramatist puts into the mouth of his heroine Helena. Here, on finding herself unexpectedly wooed by Lysander, the erstwhile lover of her friend Hermia, she exclaims, "When truth kills truth, O devilish-holy fray!" (iii.2). In this context the literal meaning of "truth" is "true love", and so the strife between the lovers is described as being at once "holy", affirmed by all the vows of heaven, and yet "devilish", owing to the disputes to which it gives rise. In the dramatic context, however, the meaning is obscure, till we reflect on the wider historical context within which the dramatist was writing his play.

Subsequently, in the problem comedy of *Measure for Measure* we come upon a more explicit mention of a religious controversy of the time concerning the compatibility between divine grace and human freedom. Not only is it more explicit, but it is much less clearly related to the dramatic context than either of the above-mentioned utterances. It is put into the mouth of the libertine Lucio in words he addresses to two anonymous gentlemen, "Grace is grace, despite of all controversy" (i.2). These words have no apparent relevance to the context in which they occur, but their relevance is rather to be found in relation to that particular controversy, as well as to the theme of "grace", which runs through many of Shakespeare's Jacobean plays. Here, however, what I wish to emphasize is that, while for Shakespeare the ideal of divine "grace" is something precious, any form of theological controversy over the ideal is, to say the least, distasteful.

The same feeling of distaste recurs in one more passage I have to quote from *Hamlet*, where the prince is accusing his mother of having been false to his father and thus having made "sweet religion" a mere "rhapsody of words" (iii.4). His reference is, like that of Helena, to the religious vows between lovers leading to the ceremony of marriage, which are reduced by the infidelity of one or the other partner to merely sweet-sounding words. At the same time, we may recognize a wider implication in the word "religion", which is "sweet" in itself and its ideal, but which is too soon reduced by controversy to nothing but "a rhapsody of words". Such were precisely the controversies spawned by Luther and other Protestant reformers, educated as they had been in the schools of Europe according to the method of logical disputation. Thanks to them and their use of the new invention of printing, the controversies which had till then been limited to the schools as a method of education, spilled over into churches, halls and even taverns. Nor were they for long limited to affairs of religion, but they also entered into the political world with disastrous consequences.

The more deeply one enters into these controversies of the Reformation both in Europe and more particularly in England, the more one realizes how central they were to the history of the sixteenth century. At the same time, one finds oneself standing at a crucial turning-point in the whole history of Western Christendom between the main divisions of "mediaeval" and "modern". Moreover, in the drama of Shakespeare one may also recognize a profound commentary on the significance of this turning-point for the culture of his time, even while he paradoxically avoids any direct mention of the religious and political forces which were at work "behind the scenes". As I have mentioned, he prudently aimed at steering clear of them, considering that, as he says through the mouth of the wily Ulysses in *Troilus and Cressida*, "There is a mystery – with whom relation / durst never meddle – in the soul of state" (iii.3). More than one dramatist of his time, such as Christopher Marlowe, had suffered for having imprudently dabbled in politics and religion in their plays, and Shakespeare was evidently resolved not to follow in their footsteps.

All the same, Shakespeare's wisdom in avoiding such subjects

– while admitting with Hamlet that this may have been "a thought which, quartered, hath but one part wisdom / and ever three parts coward" (iv.4) – need not apply to us who study his plays in the twenty-first century. We are not, I hope, in danger of being imprisoned, like Ben Jonson, or murdered, like Christopher Marlowe, for touching on these subjects, but we are merely in danger of encountering the agnostic criticism of fellow scholars. Or, as I have implied from the outset of these remarks, we may also be in danger of facing the frowns of those advocates of religious and political correctness for whom controversy, above all in matters of religion, is a forbidden subject and only ecumenical dialogue is permitted.

Such an attitude is, I grant, all very well for the twenty-first century, as a practical way of proceeding for Catholics in dealing with those of other religions or other Christian denominations. Today, it is said, we should by all means agree with each other and see each other's point of view, without betraying our own convictions. But such was, unfortunately, not the attitude of those who engaged in religious controversy during the sixteenth century, least of all in the time of Shakespeare. If Shakespeare is reluctant to touch on such matters in his plays and even expresses his distaste for such controversy, it may not necessarily have been because he was unwilling to take sides in the great religious debates of his time – as it were in the spirit of the Dutch humanist Erasmus – but because he saw how dangerous it would have been for him to do so. It may have been because, however much he may have been provoked to open his mouth on such matters, he had, like Hamlet, to keep quiet, saying, "But break, my heart, for I must hold my tongue!" (i.2). He might even have felt, like the Lady Constance in *King John*, when grieving over the fate of her son Prince Arthur, "O that my tongue were in the thunder's mouth! / Then with a passion would I shake the world!" (iii.4). It may be that is precisely, if only we knew why, what still shakes the world at performances of Shakespeare's tragedies.

Anyhow, from the standpoint of literary history, it isn't enough for us to limit our attention to the plays of Shakespeare according to their outward meaning, as dramatized versions of the stories he borrowed from his various sources such as Holinshed's *Chronicles* and Plutarch's *Lives*. That meaning is admittedly more or less secular, according to the secularity of the sources. With Shakespeare, however, as with other dramatists of his time, such as the above-mentioned Ben Jonson, we have to admit that there may well have been more in the plays than meets the eye. Such hidden meanings were by no means uncommon during the Renaissance, as the authors themselves confessed in the cases of Dante's *Divina Commedia* and Spenser's *Faery Queene*. Milton, too, speaks in his "Il Penseroso" of the "sage and solemn tunes" of great bards, "where more is meant than meets the ear". In drama, moreover, the whole institution of censorship was intended to forestall the inclusion of such double meanings as might imply any criticism of official policy.

In this context one may understand three more cryptic passages in the plays of Shakespeare. The first occurs in the early comedy of *Two Gentlemen of Verona*, in a seemingly harmless conversation between the two clowns, Speed and Launce, servants of the two gentlemen, Valentine and Proteus. When the one fails to understand the meaning of the other, Launce declares, "Thou shalt never get such a secret from me but by a parable" (ii.5). In the dramatic context this may seem to be a natural thing for him to say, but in the wider context of the age it may well conceal a hidden meaning. The same is even more strongly implied in the problem comedy of *Measure for Measure*, where it is said of the duke by Lucio, "His givings out were of an infinite distance / from his true-meant design" (i.4). The validity of applying this secretiveness to Shakespeare in the religious situation of his time may be seen partly in view of the not uncommon identification of the duke with the dramatist, partly in view of another identification proposed for the duke posing as friar with the "lurking" Jesuits of that period. Thirdly, we find something similarly secretive in the strange conversation between Lennox and another lord, when Lennox is unsure of the other's reliability and resorts to innuendo, "My former speeches have but hit your thoughts, / which can interpret further" (iii.6). This whole scene is quite unnecessary and could easily be omitted without affecting the continuity of the action, but it is significant rather of the way the dramatist is himself thinking of the religious context in these plays.

This may prompt us to look beyond the plays and their precise dramatic context to the wider context of their political and religious background. Why, we may ask, during a time when, we are assured by most historians, England has become a largely Protestant nation under the popular Virgin Queen, had there to exist such a severe censorship in matters of politics and religion, not least in the field of drama? Why was it that Shakespeare had to be so secretive in his plays, after the manner of Launce the clown, Vincentio the duke-friar, and Lennox the lord – lest he incur the fate of such fellow dramatists as Marlowe and Kyd, Nash and Jonson? Why, if not that he realizes, with Ulysses, that "there is a mystery – with whom relation / durst never meddle – in the soul of state" (iii.3)? With such a mystery, he implies, it is dangerous to meddle, if he would keep his head on his shoulders.

Now therefore it is high time for us to ask plainly, "What is this mystery?" One may trace it back to Henry VIII and his fatal decision to give himself a divorce from his first wife Catherine of Aragon and to take his mistress Anne Boleyn as his second wife, wielding the new power vested in him by a subservient Parliament as Supreme Head of the Church of England. Then he went on to make further use of this power to "reform" the Church by dissolving all the monasteries, confiscating their property and their wealth, and shamelessly pillaging it for himself and his supporters among the nobility and gentry. Though he himself remained nominally Catholic in matters of doctrine and persecuted the Lutherans in his kingdom, he failed to supervise the education of the royal children Edward and Elizabeth. The outcome was that, when they came to the throne in 1547 and 1558 respectively, they pursued a Protestant policy, even to the extent under Elizabeth of persecuting those who refused to conform and were consequently termed "recusants".

This is the situation under Queen Elizabeth, from the time of her accession to the throne in 1558, with which I now propose to deal – the situation of the religious controversies which occupied the whole of her long reign from 1558 to 1603, and which formed a considerable part of the historical background of Shakespeare. It may have been largely neglected, indeed most shamefully neglected, by Elizabethan historians and Shakespeare scholars, partly in view of Shakespeare's own seeming silence on the subject, till it has now become a subject over which a strange taboo has been cast by the modern world. Yet facts are facts, and history is history. We have to face up to the historical facts of the age, however unpleasant or even irrelevant they may seem to be whether to the present academic or modern world. Then among the historical facts in late sixteenth-century England, that is, during the reign of Queen Elizabeth, we have to admit that the religious controversies take up a central position – as may be seen from a recently published list of prisoners in the Tower of London for religious offences (cf. *The Tower of London, A Prisoner Book*, by Brian Harrison, 2004).

From the time of her accession to the throne in 1558, Elizabeth had to proceed very cautiously under the guiding hand of her chosen adviser Sir William Cecil, so as not to antagonize the substantial Catholic majority of her subjects, not to mention the many Catholic nations surrounding her country under the spiritual rule of the Pope. In her proceedings she was strangely supported by her future enemy, King Philip II of Spain, who had till recently been husband to her half-sister Mary and who now cherished the fond hope that he might now become husband also to Elizabeth. At home, the religious question was made to depend on a conference to be held at Westminster on an equal footing between the Catholic bishops and theologians from Mary's reign and the returning Protestant exiles, but the Catholic side not unnaturally refused to deal with the returning Protestants on such terms. Then not only was the conference abandoned but the Catholics were all imprisoned or kept under house arrest and forbidden to enter into any controversy on the matter of religion under what was termed a "recognizance". As a result, the Parliament that now met to decide the religious issue was enabled with a bare majority to pass the two proposed Acts of Supremacy, recognizing the Queen as "supreme governor of the Church of England", and Uniformity, accepting a common form of worship roughly according to the second Edwardian *Book of Common Prayer*.

The Protestants were now intruded into all the episcopal sees made vacant by the imprisoned Catholic bishops, and they also occupied principal places on the royal council, if by the side of not a few of the old Catholic nobility, under the Queen who now felt herself free to give expression to her Protestant preferences. At the same time, the Catholics, though they still constituted the clear majority of the English people from the time of Queen Mary, were in a state of disarray, without leaders to give them any clear guidance. The latter were now, as has been said, under the "recognizance" of silence, so long as they remained at home, or else they were living in a condition of self-imposed exile abroad.

It was in this situation, when the Catholics found themselves all of a sudden with their hands tied in the transition from the old to the new order, that a new Anglican spokesman emerged from the ranks of the returning Protestant exiles, John Jewel, the Bishop-elect of Salisbury, who now issued a challenge to the Catholics. This took the form of a sermon he delivered on three occasions, first at Paul's Cross on November 26, 1559. In it he challenged the Catholics, who had taken their stand on Tradition as opposed to the Protestant emphasis on Scripture alone, to justify certain practices accepted by their Church "out of any old Catholic doctor, or out of any old General Council, or out of the holy Scriptures of God, or any one example of the primitive Church". Such practices included those of private Mass, communion under one kind, the veneration of the real presence of Christ in the Eucharist, the ceremony of elevating the host at Mass, the veneration of images, and the prohibition of laymen to read the Bible. These were all matters which, he claimed from his study of Church history, had first been introduced into the Church during the Middle Ages.

On the other hand, how, it might be asked, were the Catholics to take up this bold challenge? The bishops were all in prison or under house arrest, and so, too, were many of their prominent theologians, who were all under "recognizance" to refrain from controversy. Others, who had made their way to the Low Countries had no means at their disposal to publish an immediate answer. When they did eventually bring out a series of published answers from their printing press at Louvain from 1564 onwards, they found, as one of Jewel's own assistants regretfully acknowledged, that Jewel himself had had every corner of the realm searched for their books, that he had had them publicly burnt at Paul's Cross, that he had procured a proclamation of the Queen against them, that he had had old men and theologians imprisoned for possessing them.

All the same, as these books succeeded in getting smuggled into the country, while the means for preventing such smuggling wasn't so elaborate as it became in later years, Jewel was obliged to bring out answers to the Catholic controversialists from Louvain – or "Lovanists", as they came to be called. Nor could he deal alone with all the replies as they increased in number from abroad, but he needed the assistance of a team both to bring out his own replies and to write other replies of their own. Indeed it turned out to be quite an industry of replies and counter-replies from both the Anglican and the Catholic side during the first decade of Elizabeth's reign, eventually totalling some ninety published items. On the Catholic side, among the many champions who came forward like David to answer the challenge of this Protestant Goliath, the most prominent was a former colleague of Jewel's from Oxford, who had for a time embraced the new teaching of Luther but had recanted under Mary, Thomas Harding.

Harding's first contribution to the controversy came out from Louvain in 1564 under the pedestrian title of *An Answer to Master Jewel's Challenge*, followed by a second edition from Antwerp in 1565. At the same time, he found that Jewel had meanwhile gone on from his *Challenge* to bring out a reasoned defence of the Anglican position against the Catholics in both Latin and English, as well for continental scholars as for English readers, respectively entitled *Apologia Ecclesiae Anglicanae* and *An Apology* or *Answer in Defence of the Church of England* in 1562. So Harding, too, felt obliged to respond with his *Confutation of a Book entitled An*

Apology of the Church of England in 1565. Such were the opening salvos in this protracted battle of books that lasted till their respective authors wearied of the task and gave up the ghost, Jewel in 1571 and Harding in 1572.

It is strange how little attention has been evoked by this "Great Controversy" among Elizabethan historians and Shakespeare scholars, and yet to Elizabethan contemporaries it was so impressive. Even in Shakespeare's day it was recalled by the learned friend of the poet Edmund Spenser, Dr Gabriel Harvey of Cambridge University, in his *Pierces Supererogation* (1593), where he speaks of Harding and Jewel as men "that deserve to have their names enrolled in the first rank of valiant confuters", whom he even compares to "our Aeschines and Demosthenes" among the great Athenian orators. He goes so far as to maintain that "scarcely any language in the Christian world hath afforded a pair of adversaries equivalent to Harding and Jewel, two thundering and lightning orators in divinity." Yet to such an extent has their estimation fallen in the modern world of learning that neither author receives so much as a mention in *The Oxford Companion to English Literature*, or even in Albert Baugh's authoritative *Literary History of England*. As for C S Lewis, who might have been expected to show more understanding of such controversial writings in his magisterial survey of *English Literature in the Sixteenth Century Excluding Drama* (1954), he blames Jewel for "the jungle of controversies to which he rashly committed himself by his so-called Challenge Sermon in 1559", while paying no attention to his Catholic opponent beyond misnaming him "John Harding". Such is the shameful situation in today's academic world!

At least, in what little space remains for me, I may give a little taste of their conflicting eloquence, so as to justify the praise deservedly accorded them by Gabriel Harvey. On his side, Jewel maintains that the Protestants have not departed from the Church of the Popes but have rather "returned to the Apostles and the old Catholic Fathers". Since their days, he continues, "all the bishops of Rome's sayings were allowed for Gospel, and all religion did only depend upon their authority." Now, however, he claims, thanks to the invention of printing and the initiative of Luther in making full use of it, "the Holy Scripture is abroad, the writings of the Apostles and the Prophets are in print, whereby all truth and Catholic doctrine may be proved," and the dreams, inventions and traditions of the so-called Catholics disproved. As for these customs and traditions, which he has listed in his Challenge, he tells his adversaries, "Let them make a proof, let them give the Gospel free passage, let the truth of Jesus Christ give his clear light and stretch forth his bright beams into all parts, and then shall they forthwith see how all these shadows will vanish and pass away at the light of the Gospel, even as the thick mist of the night consumeth at the sight of the sun."

Turning now to Harding, how, we may ask, does he defend the Catholic position against the accusations of Jewel? First, in his *Answer* he demands of the challenger what has moved him "to show such courage, to use such amplification of words, so often and with such vehemency to provoke us to encounter, and as it were at the blast of a trumpet to make your challenge?" In particular, he objects to Jewel's choice of such a limited ground for the contest, instead of dealing with matters of more importance which are the main issue between the Catholics and the Protestants. It is by means of such a stratagem, he suggests, that "craftily you shift your hands off those greater points, wherein you know Scriptures, Councils, Doctors and examples of the primitive Church to be of our side, and cast unto us, as a bone to gnaw upon, this number of articles of less weight, a few excepted, to occupy us withal." Then, coming to the end of his reply, he anticipates how Jewel and his associates will respond once they receive his *Answer*. "And now perhaps," he says, "you enter into meditation with yourself and conference with your brethren, to frame an answer to this treatise, and by contrary writing to fortify your negatives. Well may you do so. But to what purpose, I pray you? Well may you make a smoke and a smother to darken the light for a time, as men of war are wont to do to work a feat secretly against their enemies. But that cannot long continue. The smoke will soon vanish away, the light of truth will eftsoons appear."

Quite apart from the rights and wrongs of either side, and without attempting, as T S Eliot warns us in his "Little Gidding", to "revive old factions", or to "restore old policies", or to "follow an antique drum", we may well appreciate, with Dr Harvey, the remarkable eloquence revealed by both writers in defence of their respective causes. As for myself, I have to confess that in all my reading of the controversial literature on either side during the Elizabethan and the Jacobean ages, I have come across many fine examples of English prose, but few finer than these. This makes it all the more astonishing to me that such authors have been so sadly neglected on both sides, both the Anglican and the Catholic side, as well as by historians of Elizabethan literature. The extent to which this modern academic prejudice reaches is indeed appalling! Sadly, too, the same fate has befallen the other authors I might have dealt with in the course of these controversies, all of whom I have come to admire in the course of perusing their writings, even when as a Catholic and a Jesuit I disagree with their opinions.

From this point onwards there remains the further controversy between the Puritan leader Thomas Cartwright and the Anglican champion John Whitgift, both of them originally scholars of Cambridge University, though the former was obliged to spend most of his remaining life as an outcast, whereas the latter was promoted even as a result of their controversy to the dignity of Archbishop of Canterbury in 1583. Next, there comes a development of the Catholic controversy, not so much on the academic or theological as on the political issue, as to whether the many Catholic victims of the so-called Elizabethan "persecution" were to be regarded as "traitors", according to the accusation of their arch-persecutor Sir William Cecil, Lord Burghley, or as "martyrs", according to the claim made by the president of the English College at Rheims, Dr (later Cardinal) William Allen. Above all, there are the writings of the two authors who were hailed by no less a judge of prose style than Jonathan Swift as masters of English prose in the age of Shakespeare; the Jesuit Robert Persons, who was without doubt the most outstanding Catholic controversialist of his time in succession to Thomas Harding; and the great Anglican theologian, rather than controversialist, Richard Hooker. Interestingly, each of them found himself facing the growing criticism of the Puritans in such a way as to bring him and his cause closer to the other, as the Puritans came to take their stand on the basic principle of "protest", while the Anglicans fell back on Catholic positions strangely similar to those recently expounded by the great Italian champion of the Catholic cause in Rome, St Robert Bellarmine.

Chapter 4

THE RISE OF PURITANISM

Before one speaks of "the rise of Puritanism", it is necessary to know what people in general know, or think they know, about the Puritans. Most people, I suppose, think of the Puritans as men of a strict morality, refusing to indulge in such common pleasures of life as drinking and smoking and consorting with pretty girls. They are seen as men of stern appearance, like Scrooge in Dickens' *Christmas Carol*, or even Shylock in Shakespeare's *Merchant of Venice*, men whose motto is "all work and no play", in accordance with that "work-ethic" which historians after Max Weber regard as basic to the success of the industrial revolution and the rise of capitalism. Behind them lies the harsh creed of Calvinism, with its teaching of predestination, its insistence on the precise observance of the Sabbath Day and on sobriety, thrift and application to work on the other six days of the week.

Then, looking back in English history to what may be called "the golden age" of Puritanism in the seventeenth century, we may see the Puritans as the men behind the Civil War of the mid-century, when Parliament resisted the demands of King Charles I. Not that the Parliamentarians were all Puritans, though many were, but it was chiefly the Puritans who constituted the backbone of resistance to the King. At this time, we find two Puritans in particular coming to the fore, especially during the period of "the Commonwealth", the great general and leader of the so-called "roundheads" (or shock troops of cavalry), Oliver Cromwell, and the great poet and spokesman for the Puritans, John Milton. Hence a more accurate term for the Civil War would be "the Puritan rebellion".

For Americans, however, of greater importance than the Puritans who resisted King Charles I in the Civil War were those others who had previously sailed on "The Mayflower" to New England in 1620. Landing as they did on Plymouth Rock in what came to be called "the Commonwealth of Massachusetts", they became known and celebrated as "the Pilgrim Fathers", and as the founders of New England, if not of all the American colonies. They were for the most part Puritans of the strictest observance, known as separatists or Brownists (from Robert Browne of Norwich), and they refused, unlike the moderate Puritans, to recognize the Church of England as a valid Church. So they were obliged to go into exile, first to Holland and then, when they found life in Holland irksome, they set sail from Leyden in search of religious freedom for themselves (not for others) in the unknown West.

All this, however, belongs to a later phase of Puritanism, but for the origins of the movement we have to go back to the early years of Queen Elizabeth's reign, or even before to the preceding reign of Queen Mary. In the minds of most people such origins may seem obscure and therefore unimportant, but they are by no means unimportant either to Elizabethan history or to an understanding of Shakespeare's plays, which constitute the glory of that age. Yet they are commonly ignored even by Shakespeare scholars, no less than the sufferings of the English Catholics under the Elizabethan persecution. Nor is the importance of the rise of Puritanism limited to Elizabethan history or to the plays of Shakespeare. One might even say that the whole of modern Western history has been largely determined by two contemporary movements, the rise both of Puritanism and of the new science. What is more, both movements were deeply opposed to Catholic mediaeval tradition, the former to the religious tradition in the name of "Scripture", and the latter to the academic tradition in the name of "Nature".

Now, to begin at the beginning, already before Elizabeth I became Queen in 1558, during the reign of her Catholic sister Mary, many English Protestants went into exile in Germany and Switzerland, just as many English Catholics in the early years of Elizabeth found refuge in the Low Countries. Not a few of these Marian Protestants gathered at Frankfurt, as well as at Strasbourg and Geneva, but it wasn't long before there took place a schism between those who upheld the reforms enacted under Edward VI, following such leaders as Edmund Grindal, Richard Cox, and John Jewel – who all became pillars of the Elizabethan establishment – and those others who advocated the more radical reforms proposed by John Calvin, following the lead of John Knox and William Whittingham (who was also responsible for the Geneva Bible). The former (the Edwardians) looked for their ideal of reform not so much to Luther and Melanchthon at Wittenberg as to Henry Bullinger, the successor of Zwingli at Zurich. This schism was subsequently described with sad nostalgia by William Whittingham in *A Brief Discourse of the Troubles Begun at Frankfurt in Germany AD 1554*, which was published in 1575.

Here already one may see the basic points at issue between the established Church of England and the Puritans who sought a more radical reform. Not that it was just a difference between a moderate Lutheranism or Zwinglianism proposed by the former and a more extreme Calvinism urged by the latter. The difference was not so much one of theology as of Church politics. All the teachings of the reformers, including the predestinarianism of Calvin, found ready currency in Elizabethan England, and Calvin's theology in particular soon came to be regarded, at least in Elizabethan Cambridge where the Puritan scholar William Whitaker held sway as Regius Professor of Divinity, as Anglican orthodoxy. The followers of Calvin, whether in Geneva or France or Scotland, were never called "Puritans", but this was the name reserved for those English followers of Calvin who advocated his reforms not so much in theology as in ecclesiastical hierarchy and liturgy, or what they preferred to call "discipline".

The effects of the schism at Frankfurt weren't immediately apparent at the beginning of Elizabeth's reign, since it took time for liturgical conformity to be generally observed throughout the realm. For some years there was considerable discrepancy between the more traditionally minded Marian priests and the more radically disposed ministers of the new Church, concerning the rubrics or prescriptions of *The Book of Common Prayer*, which had been imposed by Act of Parliament in 1559, largely on the basis of the second Prayer Book of Edward VI in 1552. The latter in particular regarded the use of vestments, even the modified surplice and tippet, as "relics and rags of Popery" and refused to wear anything other than a university gown over their ordinary clothes. Thus when Shakespeare says, through the mouth of the clown in *Twelfth Night*, "I would I were the first that ever dissembled in such a gown" (iv.2), and when he refers, through the mouth of another clown in *All's Well That Ends Well*, to "the black gown of a big heart" (i.e. a proud heart) (i.3), he evidently has the Puritan ministers in mind.

It wasn't till 1566, however, that the Queen herself, angered at the ministers' refusal to conform in such outward matters of vesture, urged her Archbishop of Canterbury, Matthew Parker, to insist on the need of decorum in religious ceremonies. He therefore published his *Advertisement partly for Due Order in the Public Administration of Common Prayers*, not only calling for "due order" but also punishing recalcitrant ministers with deprivation of their benefices. Then the storm broke loose. Now for the first time the Puritans came out into the open, first with the publication of *A Brief Discourse against the Outward Apparel and Ministring Garments of the Popish Church*, which is generally attributed to the London minister Robert Crowley – also known as the publisher of the first printed edition of Langland's *Piers Plowman* in 1550. The controversy was soon taken up, probably by Parker himself, in *A Brief Examination for the Time of a Certain Declaration*, which was followed by another reply from the London ministers simply entitled *An Answer for the Time*. Interestingly, both sides appealed to the authority of Henry Bullinger (of Zurich) and Martin Bucer (of Strasbourg) from overseas. The ministers in particular published a whole anthology of texts from the "reverend fathers" of the Reformation entitled *The Fortress of Fathers*. What is more, all these above-mentioned books came out in the same year 1566. Also on the side of the ministers came forth a number of short letters of exhortation from various Puritan elders, such as William

Whittingham, Anthony Gilby and William Turner, author of the popular anti-Popish pamphlet, *The Hunting of the Romish Wolf* (1554). There, however, the matter rested for the time being till the death of Matthew Parker in 1575. Then the succession to the archbishopric of Canterbury went first to Edmund Grindal, who showed himself more tolerant towards the Puritans, and then to John Whitgift, under whom there took place a more vigorous renewal of the controversy from 1583 onwards.

Meanwhile, a different controversy broke out with the convening of Parliament in 1572, when the Puritans came to realize that what they were unable to effect through the clamour of printed books, they might achieve through pressure on Parliament from without and even infiltration from within. The first step in this direction was taken by two young Puritans, John Field and Thomas Wilcox, with *An Admonition to Parliament*, which they followed up with *A View of Popish Abuses yet remaining in the English Church*, and two letters from the continental reformers, Rudolph Gualter, successor of Bullinger at Zurich, and Theodore Beza, successor of Calvin at Geneva, supporting their position. Not long after, there appeared in the same year *A Second Admonition to the Parliament*, which was attributed to the Puritan leader at Cambridge, Thomas Cartwright. To this was added "An Exhortation to the Bishops and their Clergy, to answer a little book that came forth the last Parliament, and to other brethren to judge of it by God's word, until they see it answered, and not to be carried away with any respect of man."

Now at last an Anglican champion came forward in the person of John Whitgift, Master of Trinity College, Cambridge, who had already had to deal with the Puritan arguments of Cartwright, when the latter was fellow of the neighbouring St John's College as well as Lady Margaret Professor of Divinity. He now dealt with the Puritans as John Jewel before him had dealt with the Catholics overseas in the "great controversy" of the 1560s. Still in the year 1572 he published his reply to Cartwright in *An Answer to a Certain Libel, entitled An Admonition to the Parliament*. To this he added two letters from Gualter and Bullinger in support of the bishops, together with his own criticism of the above-mentioned exhortations. Now Cartwright in turn came out into the open to defend both Puritan Admonitions against the attacks of Whitgift, under the initials "T.C.", with *A Reply to an Answer made of M. Doctor Whitgift, against the Admonition to the Parliament*, in 1573. Thus the battle was formally joined by these two other great champions, the Anglican Whitgift and the Puritan Cartwright.

Then, just as the Catholics in the 1560s had been prevented by authority to continue their controversy in academic peace and freedom without the thunders of denunciations and royal proclamations from above, so now the Puritans found themselves faced in the summer of 1575 with a royal proclamation for the suppression both of the Admonitions and of Cartwright's *Reply*, while Cartwright himself was driven into exile in Germany. During his absence there appeared two Anglican answers to his *Reply*, yet another from Whitgift, entitled *The Defence of the Answer to the Admonition*, and an anonymous work with the title *A Defence of the Ecclesiastical Regiment in England*, both in 1574. Then to Whitgift's second book Cartwright, not to be outdone in pertinacity even from his exile in Germany, published his *Second Reply* in two instalments, the first in 1575 and the second in 1577.

In the course of this controversy it is interesting to observe how Shakespeare seems to draw upon it in his characterization of two "Puritans" in his plays, Shylock in *The Merchant of Venice* and Angelo in *Measure for Measure*. As for the former play, just as Shylock is said by Antonio to "cite Scripture for his purpose" (i.3), so Whitgift retorts against his Puritan opponent that heretics have the word of God "evermore in their mouth and always talk of it". Just as Shylock lays rigid emphasis on the law, so Whitgift says of Cartwright's attitude that it "smelleth of Judaism", and he demands, "What remaineth but to say that Christ is not yet come?" Again, just as Shylock refuses to eat or drink or even pray with Christians (i.3), so Whitgift declares of the Puritans in general, "These men separate themselves from our congregation and will not communicate with us neither in prayers, hearing the word, nor sacraments." As for the latter play, just as Angelo is about to sentence Claudio to death for the sin of fornication with Juliet according to an old law of Vienna (evoking the Law of Moses, which, however, limited the death sentence to sins of adultery), Cartwright defends the severity of Moses in this respect, maintaining that such sinners "should be put to death", adding, "if this be bloody and extreme, I am content to be so counted with the Holy Ghost." Whitgift, on the other hand, appeals to "the lenity of the Gospel" over "the severity of the Law", and he objects that Cartwright is bringing back the intolerable "bondage of the Law" upon Christian people.

Meanwhile, Cartwright was making full use of his German exile to elaborate "the platform of Church discipline" with his Puritan friend Walter Travers. It was apparently Travers who brought out the Latin text of their collaborative work under the title, *Ecclesiasticae Disciplinae, et Anglicanae Ecclesiae ab illa aberrationis, plena e Verbo Dei et dilucida Explicatio*, in 1574. Cartwright on his side wrote the preface and the English translation also in 1574, *A full and plain Declaration of Ecclesiastical Discipline out of the Word of God, and of the declining of the Church of England from the same.* The importance of these two works in Latin and English may not have been so evident at the time, though they were held in great respect by the Puritans at home. But the Latin text was subsequently revised under the new title of *Disciplina Ecclesiae sacra* at a general conference of the Puritans in 1586, with Cartwright's further translation as *A Directory of Church Government.* Neither document was published at the time, but the English, which was found in Cartwright's study after his death in 1603, was published during the Civil War in 1644 as a handbook for the new Presbyterian Church which was to replace the old established Church of England.

About this time, there also appear two Puritan "heresies", which were rejected one after another with civil penalties attached by the Church of England. One was a form of Anabaptism known as the Family of Love, which was imported from the Low Countries in the 1570s. Originally, it had come from Basle, but in England its principal prophet was one Henry Nicholas of Cologne, usually mentioned by his initials as "H.N." In 1574 and 1575 many of his books were translated into English by his leading representative in England Christopher Vitel, though published, it seems, in Amsterdam. Typical titles were *The Prophecy of the Spirit of Love* (1574) and *Evangelium Regni, A Joyful Message of the Kingdom* (1575). They seem to have been harmless enough, characterized throughout by biblical language, and its members were difficult to identify, as they adopted the outward appearance of conformity to the official religion. Yet it was chiefly Puritan writers, such as John Rogers and John Knewstub, who came out most strongly against them, vilifying them as "an horrible sect of gross and wicked heretics, naming themselves the Family of Love" and as teaching "monstrous and horrible heresies". More effective against them, however, was a royal proclamation, published in October 1580, with special mention of the two books of H.N. mentioned above. So they were driven underground for a time, till they reappeared in the reign of James I, only to be satirized (among others) by Ben Jonson with his *Bartholomew Fair* in the hypocritical character of Zeal-of-the-land Busy.

A second heresy was that of the Brownists, who are chiefly known from the passing remark of Sir Andrew Aguecheek in Shakespeare's *Twelfth Night*, "I had as lief be a Brownist as a politician" (iii.2). They were the more extreme kind of Puritans, who wouldn't recognize the established Church of England as a true reformed church, since it retained so many relics from the days of Popery. They were led by Robert Browne of Norwich and his associate Richard Harrison, and on account of their refusal to accept the established Church they were obliged to emigrate to Middelberg in Zeeland. From there Browne published his manifesto entitled *A Treatise of Reformation without Tarrying for Any* in 1582, with other books, and Harrison followed him in 1583. None of their writings were considered worthy of refutation, but another royal proclamation came out against them in June 1583, "against certain seditious and schismatical books and libels . . .

set forth by Robert Browne and Richard Harrison". In the same month two unfortunate disciples of theirs, Coppin and Thacker, were arrested for distributing the books and were hanged for their pains. Browne himself was back in England in 1584, after having made his peace with the church authorities and quarrelled with Harrison. He also wrote an answer to Cartwright, who had expressed his disapproval of their schism and insisted on the need of reforming the church from within.

This movement, however, took place long before Shakespeare began his dramatic career in London and his subsequent composition of *Twelfth Night*. But it continued on a small scale, from Browne and Harrison in the early 1580s, through Barrow and Greenwood in the early 1590s, till the time of the prolific Brownist author Francis Johnson with his colleague Henry Ainsworth in the mid-1590s. From 1595 onwards Johnson's divergence of opinion from the main body of English Puritans plainly appears in his *Treatise of the Ministry of the Church of England* (1595), followed by his manifesto of separatism in *A True Confession of the Faith* (1596), in which however he protested against the imputation of Brownism. The following year he chose the path of exile as separatist pastor at Amsterdam in Holland.

Meanwhile, a second vestiarian controversy had broken out with the appointment of John Whitgift as Archbishop of Canterbury in 1583. The *Advertisements* of Matthew Parker had long since remained a dead letter and the liberty of the Puritans, to use Shakespeare's phrase in *Measure for Measure*, had freely been "plucking justice by the nose" (i.3), particularly under the tolerant rule of Edmund Grindal. Whitgift, however, determined to revert to the rule of justice, by issuing certain *Articles*, with the Queen's approval, maintaining not only the Queen's authority in matters both civil and ecclesiastical but also the validity of the *Book of Common Prayer* as containing "nothing contrary to the word of God". These were now to be subscribed by all ministers of the Church of England under pain of being deprived of their livings. This time the Puritan protest wasn't limited to a few feeble pamphlets of self-justification within one year, but it was effectively organized over a period of several years by John Field till his premature death in 1588. First, against a defence of the *Articles* by Richard Cosin on behalf of the established church, a brilliant young Puritan, Dudley Fenner, brought out his *Counter-Poison* in 1584. Other pamphlets published in the same year by the Puritan printer Robert Waldegrave were: *A Dialogue concerning the Strife of our Church* by John Udall, Puritan minister at Kingston, the first of many such dialogues on the Puritan side; *A Fruitful Sermon upon the 12 chapter of the Epistle of S. Paul to the Romans*, attributed to Laurence Chaderton, a Puritan scholar at Cambridge, who was later accused of being "the foundation of Brownism"; and *The Learned Discourse of Ecclesiastical Government* written by William Fulke in 1573. This had been stayed from publication owing to the author's change of mind, till it came into the possession of John Field, who now published it without the author's permission. It became the object of refutation in the exceedingly lengthy *Defence of the Government Established in the Church of England* by the Dean of Salisbury, John Bridges (subsequently Bishop of Oxford), in 1587, covering some 1,400 pages.

This book of Bridges first drew the Puritan attack from Dudley Fenner, with his *Defence of the Godly Ministers* also in 1587, and from Walter Travers with his *Defence of the Ecclesiastical Discipline* in the following year. Also about this time the Puritans were taking active measures for the promotion of their cause in Parliament, in Convocation, in the Privy Council, and with the Queen herself. These took the form of a series of complaints, petitions, humble motions, supplications and exhortations, most of them anonymous, but published together in the Puritan *Part of a Register* in 1593. Among these petitioners one who stood out both for his name and for his zeal was the young Welshman John Penry, who first published *A Treatise containing the Equity of an Humble Supplication* to be presented before the Parliament of 1587 on behalf of the country of Wales, and secondly *An Exhortation unto the Governors and people of Wales* in 1588. This last-mentioned work now led to a strange controversy not only between Penry and an Anglican opponent, Dr Robert Some of Cambridge, but also between the latter and another Puritan champion, Job Throckmorton, MP for Warwick. Against the *Exhortation* Some brought out his first *Godly Treatise* in 1588, and then in reply to Penry's further *Defence of that which hath been written* he went on to publish a greatly enlarged edition of his *Godly Treatise*, which ran to 200 pages in contrast to the 37 pages of his first edition. Penry's place was now taken by Job Throckmorton, who came out with a masterpiece of anti-episcopal satire (also shamefully ignored by scholars) in the anonymous *M. Some laid open in his colours* in the following year. He may also be the author of the next Puritan dialogue, *Wherein is plausibly laid open the tyrannical dealing of L. Bishops against God's children*.

These Puritan writings came to a climax with the series of Martin Marprelate pamphlets, which appeared in the immediate aftermath of the defeat of the Spanish Armada in 1588. They, too, were published anonymously by the Puritan printer Robert Waldegrave. He now had to be continually on the move with his press from place to place to avoid arrest by the Anglican authorities, who as usual resorted to strong measures against their adversaries. The authorship of the pamphlets has been variously attributed to Penry, Udall and Throckmorton, who all had a hand in their publication, but the most likely candidate is Throckmorton. They began by way of satire on the bulky tome of John Bridges, with two pamphlets respectively known as *The Epistle* and *The Epitome*, which are at first hard to tell apart from each other since they both have the same long title beginning, *Oh Read over D. John Bridges*. The first was published at East Molesey by the River Thames in October 1588, and the second at Fawsley in Northamptonshire in November. They were followed by a brief broadside entitled *Certain Mineral and Metaphysical Schoolpoints*, printed at Coventry in January 1589. More than any previous Puritan publications, they were characterized by a vein of scurrilous criticism against the Anglican bishops, descending to libels on their personal lives.

The counter-attack of the bishops was led by Thomas Cooper, Bishop of Winchester, in the dignified form of *An Admonition to the People of England* in 1589. This, however, only elicited two more scurrilous pamphlets from Martin, addressing himself to Cooper by name, with punning reference to a common street-cry, *Hay Any Work for Cooper?*, which was also printed at Coventry in March 1589, and *More Work for Cooper*, which was seized at Manchester in August and destroyed. Another Anglican reply was delivered by Richard Bancroft, who now emerged as the right-hand man of Whitgift and the principal hammer of the Puritans, typically relying on both forceful and literary methods of refutation. His first attack took the form of a *Sermon Preached at Paul's Cross the 9 of February*, which is also notable for its defence, the first of its kind on the Anglican side, of the apostolic and divine origin of episcopacy. A few days later, on February 13, he was supported by a royal proclamation enforcing his criticism of "certain seditious and schismatical books and libels". There followed three more tracts in the Marprelate series, *Theses Martinianae*, *The Just Censure*, and *The Protestation of Martin Marprelate*, before they were finally discontinued in September 1589, all of them having been printed at Wolston in Warwickshire. Already, however, by the May and June of 1589, Martin was being assailed by attacks of the same scurrilous kind as he himself had used. For them Bancroft had turned to the dramatists of the time, the so-called "university wits", in particular John Lyly, Robert Greene and Thomas Nash. Their pamphlets were variously entitled *Pap with an Hatchet*, *An Almond for a Parrot*, and *Pasquil's Apology*, but which author wrote which pamphlet remains something of a puzzle. Mostly they fizzled out after 1590. Only the name of "Marprelate" survives in that of the self-righteous parson in Shakespeare's *As You Like It*, Sir Oliver Martext.

These pamphlets led to yet another strange controversy between two literary figures of the time, the above-mentioned Dr Gabriel Harvey, also famous for his association with the poet Edmund Spenser, and the "university wit" Thomas Nash, both of them from Cambridge. First, Gabriel's Puritan brother Richard sought to make peace between the warring parties with a well-intentioned work, *Plain Perceval, the Peace-maker of England* (1590), followed shortly by *A Theological Discourse of the Lamb of God* (also 1590), but he only drew down on himself the derision of Robert Greene in *A Quip for an Upstart Courtier* (1592). Since Greene was attacking not only Richard but also Gabriel Harvey, the latter now joined in the dispute with his *Four Letters* (also 1592). Now, not content with criticizing Greene, who had just died – shortly after his famous warning against the young Shakespeare as "an upstart crow, beautified with our feathers", in his *Groatsworth of Wit*, also 1592 – Gabriel attacked Nash, who had recently published his *Pierce Penniless* and went on to reply to Harvey in his *Strange News*. In this way, one work led to another in a crabbed style which is all but incomprehensible to modern readers on account of the many ephemeralities of the controversy. In sum these writings – and I have only mentioned a few of them – contributed no less than the Marprelate tracts to what T S Eliot calls the "inspissation" of English prose towards the end of the Elizabethan age and the rise of Shakespearian drama. Even the personalities on either side have been discerned, not without a wealth of conflicting evidence, in the characters of the ponderous pedant Holofernes (for Dr Gabriel Harvey) and the witty page Moth (for Thomas Nash) in Shakespeare's *Love's Labour's Lost*.

The tragic outcome to all these frivolous controversies may be seen in the fate of two of the Martinists, John Penry and John Udall, who were both sentenced to death for their parts in bringing out the pamphlets – though Udall was granted a reprieve, only to die in prison a year or two later. It may also be seen in the fate of the two separatists, Henry Barrow and John Greenwood, who both suffered the extreme penalty of death, though they had no proven connection with Marprelate, but only with the writings of Robert Browne. While in prison, Barrow produced a manifesto of his revived Brownist movement, entitled *A True Description out of the Word of God of the visible Church*, in 1589, only to be attacked by the indefatigable Dr Some in his third *Godly Treatise* of 1589. He also wrote *A Brief Discovery of the False Church*, to be printed at Dort in Holland, but the edition was confiscated and used by his judges as incriminating evidence against him at his trial in 1593. As for Job Throckmorton, though he had probably been behind both the mind and the pen of Martin Marprelate, he was never convicted, perhaps because of his genteel connections, though he was openly accused of complicity by the Anglican Dean of Exeter, Matthew Sutcliffe, in his *Answer unto a Certain Calumnious Letter* of 1595.

The major outcome to all the Anglican-Puritan controversies, however, was the emergence of the one really great Anglican champion, greater than either John Jewel in the 1560s or John Whitgift in the 1570s, Richard Hooker. He had begun his scholarly life at Jewel's college in Oxford, Corpus Christi, and there he would have preferred to remain till the end of his reclusive days, but that his assistance was required by Whitgift for the anti-Puritan controversy. Only, his method of conducting controversy wasn't the harsh method of Whitgift, nor the forceful method of Bancroft, nor yet the more scurrilous method of Sutcliffe, still less the satirical, libellous method of Martin Marprelate himself or the "university wits" opposing him. He was by preference more of a theologian than a controversialist, and he was now led to shore up the theological foundations of the Church of England against the attacks chiefly of Travers and Cartwright, in a series of seven volumes entitled *The Laws of Ecclesiastical Polity*. The first four volumes of this work were published together in 1593-94, and a fifth volume, longer than all the preceding ones, followed in 1597. The remaining two were, however, destroyed by his shrewish Puritan wife, before he himself died in 1600. Just before that date some Puritans ventured to criticize his great work in what they entitled *A Christian Letter of Certain English Protestants*, one of whom was almost certainly Thomas Cartwright. Interestingly enough, he was criticized not only for his elaborate Ciceronian style, which was so different from the plain style recommended by the Puritans, but also for his arguments, for which he drew not so much on the Protestant reformers as on the Catholic schoolmen Aquinas and Scotus. After his death, he was defended by his friend William Covell, who published *A Just and Temperate Defence of the Five Books of Ecclesiastical Polity* in the last year of the old reign, 1603.

Finally, in connection with the *Laws*, one may point to its probable influence on the later plays of Shakespeare, not least his tragic masterpieces, *Hamlet* and *King Lear*. This probability has been emphasized by two American scholars, Virgil Whitaker in his *Shakespeare's Use of Learning* (1953) and Roy Battenhouse in his *Shakespearean Tragedy, Its Art and Its Christian Premises* (1973). As for myself, when I came to study Shakespeare's plays at Oxford in 1952, I had devoted three years to the study of Thomist philosophy, and I felt it an appropriate step from the thought of Aquinas to the poetry and drama of Shakespeare. I even went on to contribute an article on the influence of Aquinas on Shakespeare for a journal named *Studies in Mediaeval Thought*, in commemoration of the Shakespeare centenary in 1964. At that time I hadn't yet come across Whitaker's book, and I could only wonder how Shakespeare might have familiarized himself with the works of Aquinas. The similarity was there for sure, but was it, I wondered, merely an accident of great minds thinking alike? Once, however, I came upon Whitaker's book, I could recognize the point of contact between the minds of Aquinas and Shakespeare by way of Hooker. Then I went on to devote part of a chapter to Hooker in my study of *Shakespeare's Religious Background* (1973).

Anyhow, there I may leave the story of the early rise of Puritanism with the end of the Elizabethan age, before it emerges more openly onto the stage of history. Already on its way through the minor controversies of the Elizabethan age, one may see how it led, by way of the Brownists and other separatists, to the historic voyage of the Pilgrim Fathers and then, by way of the "discipline" of Cartwright and Travers, to the Puritan rebellion and the replacement of the old Anglican with a new Presbyterian church. At the same time, I must add, it all helped to fashion the dramatic genius of William Shakespeare.

Chapter 5

SHAKESPEARE AND
THE REFORMATION

To what extent, it may be asked (though it is a surprisingly uncommon question to be asked), was Shakespeare influenced in his dramatic composition by the events of the English Reformation? It may also be asked why this question is so surprisingly uncommon. After all, the age of Shakespeare and his parents was that of the Reformation in England, as initiated by Henry VIII in his desire of a divorce from Catherine of Aragon and consummated by his daughter Elizabeth I. Yet in the plays of Shakespeare there seems to be so little by way of comment on these great events of his time, at least from the viewpoint of religion, though in other respects, as Hamlet says of plays and players, they are "the abstracts and brief chronicles of the time" (ii.2).

Two reasons may be given for this apparent absence of comment on the great religious issues of the time. The first may be found in an early royal proclamation against the abuse of the stage for religious propaganda on either side, as had been the case during the previous reigns of Henry VIII, Edward VI and Mary. It is to this proclamation that we may trace the sudden change from a religious drama that had prevailed through the late Middle Ages to a secular drama in the age of Elizabeth. For this reason the drama of Shakespeare is by no means uniquely secular, but he shares his seeming secularity with all the contemporary dramatists in England.

Secondly, insofar as he does comment, if only indirectly, on the religious controversies which continued unabated during the reigns of both Elizabeth I and James I, one may point to three remarks in his plays (mentioned at greater length in a preceding chapter) which indicate a distaste for such disputation. In each case the remark is oddly out of context and might easily have been omitted without detriment to the sequence of thought in the scene where it occurs. Thus in *Romeo and Juliet*, Mercutio's dying curse on "both your houses" of Montague and Capulet (iii.1) might well have been applied in the minds of an Elizabethan audience to the protagonists on either side of the religious divide. Again, in the contemporary comedy of *A Midsummer Night's Dream*, Helena's complaint against a situation, "where truth kills truth" in "a devilish-holy fray" (iii.2), more aptly refers to religious controversy than to lovers' quarrels. Thirdly, in *Measure for Measure*, when Lucio observes that "Grace is grace, despite of all controversy" (i.2), he is evidently alluding to contemporary disputes among both Catholics and Protestants on the subject of "grace", but such an allusion has little relevance to the dramatic context. In other words, what is common to all three remarks is a reference not so much to anything in the play as to the outside world of the dramatist and his audience.

One might therefore say that, on the surface of the plays as dramatized versions of the stories on which they are based, the dramatist seems to be maintaining a resolutely secular stance, while keeping the disputed topic of religion at arm's length. It is as if, amid the religious oppositions of his time, he means to avoid all partisanship in order to appeal to the hearts of all members of his audience, whatever their religious persuasions might be. Then, it may further be asked, does this mean that the dramatist is indifferent to religion as such, or to the Christian religion in particular, in a desire to rise above all differences of creed? Not necessarily, one may answer, any more than (say) Erasmus in his day succeeded in keeping aloof from the quarrel between Luther and the supporters of the Pope (including Henry VIII). After all, one doesn't have to be irreligious to disapprove of disputes about religion. Rather, such disapproval might well arise, as we may see in Shakespeare's plays for another, deeper reason, from a deep attachment to what he calls, in Hamlet's words, "sweet religion" (iii.4).

What then, it may yet again be asked, is this other, deeper reason in the plays by which Shakespeare may be said to reveal his attachment to religion? Well, common to all sides in the religious controversies of the sixteenth century, whether Protestant, Puritan or Papist – to use the alliterated forms of the "three religions" recognized at that time – was a respect for and an appeal to the authority of the Bible. Not that Shakespeare ever appeals to this authority in his plays, or if he does, he is as likely as not to put the appeal into the mouth of some such "villain" as Richard III or Shylock or Falstaff, but he is always drawing on the rich language of the Bible – more than any other dramatist of his time – to lend an added depth of meaning to his plays. In the eyes of a superficial critic like George Bernard Shaw he may seem to have had "no conscious religion", "no philosophy to expound" and "no intellectually coherent drama", but that is only because his religion, his philosophy and his whole intellectual position is both biblical and traditional without any individual elaboration. Like Edgar in *King Lear*, he may be said to speak what he feels, not what he ought to say (v.3).

The extraordinary thing about Shakespeare's use of the Bible, as contrasted with that of his great rival, the Puritan John Milton, isn't so much how frequent or abundant it is, as how naturally and spontaneously, if not unconsciously, it comes to his mind and is poured into his plays. Many scholars have undertaken to identify all such allusions, but even when they limit their attention to those whose authenticity is beyond question, there remains a vast penumbra of possible allusions, of which the dramatist must surely have been aware in the moment of composition. What is more, it isn't enough to identify such allusions as constituting the presence of biblical influence in the plays, but it is also necessary to consider how far in a particular play, such as *A Midsummer Night's Dream*, they may be seen to converge as pervasive themes and grow, as Hippolyta says of the lovers' "story of the night", to "something of great constancy" (v.1).

This may be said in varying ways and to varying degrees of all Shakespeare's plays – of some more than others, yet of all both separately and when taken together – that beneath their seemingly secular surface there is a deep undercurrent of religious and biblical meaning, flowing through the earlier plays and gathering to a greatness in the four great tragedies. The biblical drama of the Middle Ages may have been driven underground owing to Protestant hostility by the time Shakespeare entered upon his dramatic career in London, but its continuance underground is apparent from the beginning not least in the early historical plays, in the mouth not only of a hypocritical villain like Richard III but also of the "pious King" Henry VI. It is as if part of Shakespeare's aim as a dramatist was, in the words of T S Eliot, to shore all these fragments of the Bible against the ruins of his English heritage.

If, for example, we take the story of Christ's Passion, which formed the central subject of the mediaeval biblical drama, and as it is still continued once every ten years at Oberammagau in Germany, we find it no less central to the great tragedies of Shakespeare. Thus the particular episode of the betrayal of Jesus by Judas with a kiss forms no insignificant undercurrent of imagery in the two tragedies of *Othello* and *Macbeth*, and the other episode of Pilate washing his hands is also echoed in *Macbeth*, if with additional echoes from Seneca and Sophocles. What is more, both these episodes evidently come to the dramatist's mind not only directly from the Bible, or from his childhood memory of the Passion plays at Coventry, but also from his previous use of them in the historical "tragedies" of *Richard III* and *Richard II*. Moreover, the Gospel account of the death of Christ on the cross and the piercing of his side with a lance, as well as the traditional image of him being laid in the arms of his sorrowing mother (in what is called the *Pietà*), may be perceived only just beneath the surface of the final Act of *King Lear* and contributing powerfully to its pathos.

Here surely is to be found the secret, all too often overlooked by Shakespeare scholars in their concern to keep religion out of literature, of Shakespeare's dramatic genius. Much as we may insist in our secular age on the need of keeping Church and State, religion and literature, apart from each other, they can hardly be kept apart in the heart of human beings, least of all in such a religious age as that of Shakespeare. Whatever may be the appearances of secularism on the surface of the plays, enforced as they were by the circumstances of the age, Shakespeare is always warning us in them, as in *The Merchant of Venice*, against the danger of being misled by these appearances, as symbolized by the caskets of gold and silver. Once we go on to allow for the pervading presence not only of biblical allusions but also of the deeper biblical themes, we may be astonished to find the plays being turned upside-down before our wondering gaze, and then the plots, which seemed to claim our prior attention, may come to take a second place to those unobtrusive biblical meanings.

Now, however, we have to confront a further question, leading to a third layer of meaning in the plays, while returning to the vexed question of the dramatist's religious allegiance. It is that, given his widely recognized Catholic upbringing both at his parents' home in Warwickshire and in recusant Lancashire, together with his evident concern for such human values as justice and mercy, he could hardly have remained unaffected by the plight of the persecuted English Catholics throughout his lifetime. Surely it isn't to be dismissed as "partisan" to discern in his plays a sympathy for them, especially when the plays themselves seem to be pointing in that direction. Was Shakespeare himself a Catholic during this period? We may not know for certain, and in any case the question hardly means anything, when it was so difficult even for convinced Catholics to practise their faith. Certainly, if Shakespeare was a convinced Catholic, he would have done his best not to reveal the fact, lest a "suborned informer", such as he dismisses in Sonnet cxxv, should accuse him to the authorities. At least, it may be said that he was aware of what was happening to the Catholics of his time, both clerical and lay, and of this awareness we find evidence in almost all his plays.

Again, as in the case of biblical influence, I can hardly be expected to mention within a brief space all the echoes in the plays of the conditions of those poor persecuted Catholics. It may be sufficient to take a few representative plays and show how clearly in their main lines they reflect those conditions. Such, for example, is the plight of the poor merchant of Syracuse, Aegeon, in *The Comedy of Errors*, who is shipwrecked on the coast of Ephesus and condemned to death for no other crime than his place of origin. What, one might think, an incredible fate! Could it have ever been the case in historical reality? Yet it was the real fate of Catholic priests coming to England during the reign of Queen Elizabeth, often disguised as merchants and as often as not with no other purpose than the spiritual assistance of their fellow-Catholics. The whole plot of the play, with all its farce and fun, springs out of just such a tragic situation. Even in the final scene, when the merchant is led out for his execution, an interesting parallel is indicated in the martyrdom of a seminary priest named William Hartley in the year of the Armada.

Then there is the more famous merchant Antonio in the comedy of *The Merchant of Venice*. His similar sadness in the opening scene is not unrelated to that of Catholic priests on arriving in London, where that city may not improbably be compared to Venice, and the Puritan city fathers to the Jewish money-lender Shylock. More precisely, his sadness is due to the forthcoming departure of his friend Bassanio for Belmont beyond the sea, which he is about to finance with money borrowed at the risk of his life. Such, too, was the situation of many a Catholic priest in England, inasmuch as their concern wasn't just to provide spiritual comfort for the Catholic laity but also, with a view to the future of the English mission, to send promising young men for their religious education to France and the Low Countries, to Spain and Rome. So when Antonio is arrested and imprisoned at the suit of Shylock, he is not insignificantly described as "one in whom the ancient Roman honour" appears (iii.2).

Turning from the main plot of "the pound of flesh" to the related plot of "the three caskets", one can hardly peruse the scene of Bassanio's choice without some sense of its topical implications. What, we may wonder, is the point of all this word-play on "the rack" and "treason" and "confession" in the setting of what Portia calls "these naughty times"? What, if not an elaborate series of barely disguised allusions to the fate attending many a Catholic priest once he is caught and imprisoned in the Tower of London. This is further emphasized by Bassanio when he goes on to speak of the danger of being deceived by "the outward shows", among which he makes special mention of "the seeming truth which cunning times put on / to deceive the wisest" (iii.2).

Such riddling reference to those familiar tortures inflicted on Catholic priests year after year in the Tower during the reign of Elizabeth, and associated with the gallows on Tyburn near what is now Marble Arch at the Western end of Oxford Street – or what Shakespeare elsewhere calls "the shape of love's Tyburn that hangs up simplicity" (*Love's Labour's Lost* iv.3) – recurs again and again in the plays, imparting a strange grimness to a seemingly light-hearted setting. There is, for instance, in *King John* the odd comment of the Bastard on Lewis the Dauphin's profession of delight in Blanch of Castile, who has just been offered to him as bride, "Drawn in the flattering table of her eye! / Hanged in the frowning wrinkle of her brow! / And quartered in her heart! He doth espy / himself love's traitor" (ii.1). Also in *Much Ado About Nothing* we come upon the no less discourteous comment of Claudio when, in response to Benedick's complaint of toothache, followed by Don Pedro's "Draw it!" and Benedick's "Hang it!" he caps them with the tasteless pun, "You must hang it first and draw it afterwards" (iii.2).

Above all, we may note a series of plays featuring a political contrast between an old and a new order, with an implicit preference of the old over the new. Such is the comedy of *As You Like It*, in which the good characters of the play are successively driven from the court and the city to the remote Forest of Arden (evocative for Shakespeare both of his home in Warwickshire and of his mother's maiden name). Here the very words used by the usurping Duke Frederick in banishing his niece Rosalind seem to echo the other words used by Lord Burghley to justify what he calls in the title of a book published in 1583, "The Execution of Justice in England", particularly on seminary priests and Jesuits. Such, too, is the problem play of *Hamlet*, where we are shown the young prince awkwardly caught between the two orders. On coming home to Denmark from the Lutheran University of Wittenberg (founded as late as 1502), he finds himself faced with a new political order which has many parallels with the Elizabethan state but with which he finds himself at variance, tied as he is to the old order by his father's ghost. No small part of Hamlet's inner contradiction, which may have been shared by his creator, is the way he feels himself torn between the ideology of Lutheran reform, the harsh reality of a Denmark which resembles the Elizabethan state, and his primary allegiance to the Catholic past.

Such, finally, is the saddest of Shakespeare's tragedies, *King Lear*, in which it is the old King who wilfully, or as Gloucester puts it "on the gad" (i.2), banishes his one good daughter Cordelia with the loyal Kent and entrusts himself to the care of his two false daughters. There follows a situation which is oddly reminiscent of *As You Like It*, in which the good characters are all disinherited and driven into exile. In particular, the characterisation of Kent and Edgar and their respective assumption of disguise, for the sake the one of the King and the other of his father, is remarkably similar to the proscribed condition of the hunted priest in Elizabethan England – even in such details as the giving out of "proclamations", the watch kept at "all ports" and the threat of "intelligence" (or information gleaned by spies). Such topical allusions may not amount to a full-scale allegory of the Catholic condition in England, but at least they serve to show how far that condition was preying on the dramatist's mind. Then perhaps, even without an intention to develop the parallel, it may have forced itself on the dramatist's attention. In this way he adds a third layer of meaning to his plays, beneath not only the secular surface of the plots he has derived from various sources, but also the biblical language and themes by which he deepens his dramatic interpretation of those plots. This he develops by means of a subtle but insistent reference to the harsh situation of so many innocent Catholics, though they were only trying to remain faithful to a religion which had till but recently been that of all Englishmen for close on a thousand years.

In conclusion, therefore, in response to the question, "What was the impact of the English Reformation on the plays of Shakespeare?" I can only say it was immense. Putting it simply, without the Reformation we wouldn't have had any of his plays. This isn't to say, however, that he was in agreement with that movement, whether in the religious or the political sense. Rather, we see him affected by it in a negative sense, in that he aims at closing his eyes to the religious disputes of his time by adopting a secular stance, while at the same time, drawing on its positive contribution to the English language through the various biblical translations of the period, which he uses to lend depth of meaning to the stories he takes from his sources. Above all, we may further discern a deeper level of inspiration and indignation, which he feels as an Englishman and a human being, at the injustices and cruelties inflicted on his fellow English and fellow Catholics for no other crime than that of refusing to go along with an upstart government in abandoning the religion which had commanded the loyalty and affection of generations of his countrymen since the time of Saint Augustine. As for those Shakespeare scholars who refuse to recognize this reality at the heart as well of the plays as of the age, they may best be described in the words of Jesus as "the blind leading the blind".